Twenty-one Plays
for Children

Pelham Moffat, born in 1895 in Edinburgh, started work in business, and after losing an arm in the First World War he resumed his former occupation. Through a study of Rudolf Steiner's writings he became increasingly interested in education. After taking an honours degree at Edinburgh University he was instrumental in founding the Rudolf Steiner School of Edinburgh in 1939.

It was during the following twenty-six years of teaching that he wrote the plays published here. He died in 1976.

Pelham S. Moffat

Twenty-one Plays for Children

Floris Books

First published in 1967 by Edinburgh
Rudolf Steiner School Trust Ltd
Reprinted in 1989 by Floris Books

© Estate of Pelham S. Moffat 1967
All rights reserved. No part of this book may
be reproduced without the prior permission of
Floris Books, 21 Napier Road, Edinburgh

British Library CIP Data available

ISBN 0-86315-094-2

Printed in Great Britain
by Billing & Sons, Worcester

CONTENTS

Introduction	7
Saint Francis and the Wolf (*age 7–8*)	9
Joseph and his Brethren (*age 8–9*)	13
The Last Plague (*age 8–9*)	29
Saul (*age 8–9*)	33
Christmas Play (*age 8–9*)	42
The Death of Baldur (*age 9–10*)	51
Thor and the Giants (*age 9–10*)	63
The Wise Men's Well (*age 9–10*)	71
Gilgamesh and Eabani (*age 10–11*)	79
The Hall of Judgment (*age 10–11*)	88
The Return of Odysseus (*age 10–11*)	101
Romulus and Remus (*age 11–12*)	114
The Emperor's Vision (*age 11–12*)	122
Dorothea (*age 11–12*)	126
Cornelia (*age 11–12*)	136
The Death of Julius Caesar (*age 11–12*)	149
St. Columba (*age 12–13*)	167
Wind on the Waters (*age 12–13*)	174
Christopher Columbus (*age 12–13*)	181
After Battle (*age 13–14*)	189
Bonny Justice (*age 13–14*)	200
Le Petit Paresseux (*age 9*)	212
Au Café (*age 12–13*)	214
La Tante Hélène (*age 12–13*)	216

INTRODUCTION

The following plays were written over a period of years for children of the Rudolf Steiner School of Edinburgh in connection with work being done in various classes during that time; and although they were written for this specific purpose, it has been suggested that they might possibly be of use not only to teachers in other Rudolf Steiner Schools, but to teachers generally, in fact, to anyone occupied with young people. All the plays—apart from the two Christmas plays and one of the French sketches—have been publicly performed, i.e. in a hall or theatre outside the school premises, some on several occasions, and always by children of the ages indicated. There is no need of course to adhere strictly to the ages given, but provided the interest of the children has been aroused in the story from which any particular play has been derived, it will be found that these ages are most suitable. The age-range is from 7 to 14. After 14 children are normally becoming old enough to attempt adult plays, but the plays included here for children of age 12 upwards might well be performed by young adolescents. Their acting would of course be more mature. Nevertheless it must not be thought that children of the ages indicated here are too young to give quite moving performances such as the writer has experienced many times. The all-important thing is, that the feelings of the children should first be stirred by the story as told by the teacher (not read). Then, during rehearsals, if the teacher is prepared to jump into any part and show a child how a passage should be spoken and acted, the child will "catch on" to the part. Nearly every child needs some demonstration of this kind,—not that he should merely imitate the teacher, for that would not be acting—but so that the idea of the part "lights up" in him.

The plays, commencing with legend, move into the historical at age 12. Up to age 10-11 the plays are written in rhyme, this being most suitable for these years. In the following year blank verse is introduced, and for the last two years (with one exception) they are in prose. The plays are so constructed that in the earlier years there is always a chorus. In fact, the first play, "St. Francis and the Wolf", has really only one individual part. As the children grow older the chorus becomes less dominant and more individual parts arise, while by age 11-12 this element disappears altogether.

The author has always found that the best way for younger children to learn a play is for the whole class to speak it at first in chorus (including any individual parts) repeating a few lines at a time first spoken by the teacher. It is amazing how quickly the children learn the whole play in this fashion. Then individual children can be selected to perform the separate parts on their own. At age 11–12 however, transcriptions of the parts can suitably be handed to the children to be read at rehearsals and even learned at home, if necessary.

As the school in which these plays were written is co-educational, there are parts for both boys and girls. In Primary State schools this should provide no difficulty, but in schools which are not co-educational it is quite common for female parts to be taken by boys, or male parts by girls.

Teachers in other Rudolf Steiner schools will of course recognise at once how these plays follow the curriculum. For non-English speaking Rudolf Steiner schools abroad it is hoped that the plays might be helpful in English lessons.

The author is convinced that it is of great educational value for children to be able to enter deeply with their feelings into a play—whether legendary or historical—provided the story has some real moral and aesthetic significance. Not that a moral should be pointed at, or in any way underlined; but a serious moral element should underlie everything they act. They should never be asked to perform anything trivial. In this way we help to educate their feelings. If we paid as much attention to the education of feeling in young children as we do to the cultivation of intellectual cleverness, we should not see so much feeling and emotion running riot in adolescence. Finally, as the lines of a play have to be repeated many times by the children, in the course of rehearsal, it is also important that the language of the play should be as melodious as possible, and particularly that the verse they are asked to repeat should come as near to poetry as one is capable of writing. The author has always been deeply conscious of this responsibility towards the children in writing each play, and he has done his best to strive towards these standards.

SAINT FRANCIS AND THE WOLF

(age 7–8)

This is taken from the well-known legend regarding St. Francis of Assisi and the wolf of Gubbio. The people of Gubbio form the chorus, there is a watchman who has a few lines to say, St. Francis himself, and the Wolf who has nothing to say apart from a long, fierce howl. Such a simple play needs no scenery.

The story can be found in "The Little Flowers of St. Francis" and in most books of legends of the Saints.

CHORUS: Francis, friend of beast and bird
    Bade them listen to his word—
    Brother wolf and sister mouse
    Sharers of the self-same house—
    Covered by a roof of blue,
    Carpeted with moss and dew,
    While the window of the sun
    Sheds its light on everyone.
    Thus he taught the birds to give
    Thanks to God by Whom they live,
    Tamed the fiercest beast of prey,
    Teaching him a gentler way.

(Enter Francis)

    As he journeyed through the land,
    Neither scrip nor staff in hand,
    Came he, when the sun was low,
    By the town of Gubbio.

WATCHMAN: What ho! friend, you travel late!

CHORUS: Cries the watchman at the gate.

WATCHMAN: See! the sudden shadows drop
    From the flaming mountain-top.

          Tarry with us till the day
          Comes to light you on your way.

FRANCIS: Thank you for your welcome warm.
          Do you fear a coming storm?

WATCHMAN: Ah, sir, little do you know
          Of the town of Gubbio.
          When the evening hour is late
          None dares venture through the gate;
          For the wolf, in shadows black,
          Haunts the tardy traveller's track.

FRANCIS: Brother wolf? so fierce and wild
          That he murders man and child!
          Sad the news you have to tell!
          For your care I thank you well.
          I have wandered many a mile
          And would gladly rest awhile.

CHORUS: Francis listened to the woe
          Of the folk of Gubbio,
          Sat with head in sorrow bent:—

FRANCIS: God has sent this punishment.
          You have suffered this distress
          For your people's wickedness.
          But, be sorry for your sin,
          Then will peaceful days begin.
          Lead me to this monster grim.
          I would gladly speak with him.

PEOPLE: To the wolf? We should not dare!
          Only death awaits you there.

FRANCIS: Death? Why should you feel alarm?
          I have never done him harm.
          Why should brother wolf harm me?
          Show me where his dwelling be.

PEOPLE: Then, with trust in help Divine,
          Francis made the holy sign,

And the people watched him go
Through the gates of Gubbio.
Followed after, sore afraid,
Saw him walking undismayed
To the wood upon the hill.
Fearfully they followed still.
Suddenly the wolf they saw
Rush on him with gaping jaw.

FRANCIS: Hither, brother wolf, to me!
In God's name I summon thee!
And command thee, by His Son,
Hurt not me nor anyone.

(The wolf approaches)

Brother wolf, thy wicked ways
Make these men thine enemies.
But if thou wilt promise still
Nevermore to hurt or kill,
They will all thy sins forgive
And will pledge, that while thou live,
They will *give* to thee instead
Every day thy daily bread.
Brother, wilt thou promise me
This to do most faithfully?

PEOPLE: Then the people wond'ring saw
Brother wolf put forth his paw,
Gently lay it in his hand
That the saint might understand,
Then obedient, meek and slow
Follow him to Gubbio.
See the crowding folk rejoice,
Praising God with gladsome voice,
While the wolf for evermore
Begs his bread from door to door.

CHORUS: Francis, friend of beast and bird
Bade them listen to his word—

Brother wolf and sister mouse
Sharers of the self-same house—
Covered by a roof of blue,
Carpeted with moss and dew,
While the window of the sun
Sheds its light on everyone.

JOSEPH AND HIS BRETHREN

(age 8–9)

The next three plays are concerned with stories from the Old Testament, and that of Joseph and his Brethren is surely one of the most beautiful in all literature. It is in every way complete; it has simple human tragedy, moments of intense drama, and a wonderful unfolding in which wickedness is deflected into a far-reaching good, while the offenders, being brought to a realisation of their own deeds, are amazed to meet with mercy. To live in this story by acting it is a marvellous experience for children of this age, teaching them many things without a word being spoken. But the whole story should first be told, over several days, so that it really reaches their feelings.

The characters are here more individualised and the play is an exception among those for the younger children in that it has no chorus. It was written originally for a small group of children and what would have been the work of a chorus is here undertaken by a single voice linking the scenes by passages from the Old Testament. These can of course be read. Again, apart from one or two properties, this play needs no scenery.

SCENE I

JOSEPH: My brethren, I have dreamed a dream—
    'Twas autumn, and the fields did seem
    Aglow with waving harvest gold,
    As we went reaping—and behold,
    Each with a sickle in his hand
    We reaped the first-fruits of the land.
    A single sheaf we bound, each one,
    And laid it in the shining sun,
    When lo, the sheaf I newly bound
    Stood upright on the stubble ground,
    While yours—as to a king divine—
    Arose, and bowed themselves to mine.

1ST BROTHER (Judah): What idle tale is this to bring?
    Shall we be servants, thou a king?

2ND BROTHER (Reuben): Shalt thou, our younger brother, thus
    Have dominion over us?

3RD BROTHER (Simeon): He dreameth things he cannot do,
    And hopeth that his dream be true!

JOSEPH: My father, they so angry seem!
    I did but tell them of a dream!

JACOB: My son, to me thy dreams impart,
    And I shall keep them in my heart.

JOSEPH (*sits*): I dreamed, my father, yet again—
    Not of the corn, or sheaves, or men—
    I stood upon the floor of heaven
    And sun and moon and stars eleven
    Unto me obeisance made.

JACOB: My son, my son, what hast thou said?
    Shall I, thy mother, brethren,—all
    Upon the earth before thee fall?

4TH BROTHER: No matter. Let him dream his fill!
    We to the sheep upon the hill—
    And farther shall we haply go
    Where-e'er the greenest grasses grow.

5TH BROTHER: Until we come again, farewell!
    Thou mayst have other dreams to tell!

1ST BROTHER (*as they march out*): The sun and moon and stars, no less!

    (*stops and turns round*)

3RD BROTHER: Clothed in his many-coloured dress!

    (*They go out*)

READER: And his brethren went to feed their father's flock in Shechem. And Israel said unto Joseph. Do not thy brethren feed the flock in Schechem? Come, and I will send thee unto them. Go now, see whether it be well with thy brethren, and well with the flock; and bring me word again.

    (*Exit* JOSEPH)

SCENE II

4TH BROTHER: This pasture's good, here let us lie
 And watch the noon-day hours go by.

(Sits)

2ND BROTHER: And there's a well of water deep
 A place to gladden men and sheep!

3RD BROTHER *(looking in)*:
 Much gladness may thou draw from it!
 The well is dry—an empty pit.

5TH BROTHER: No matter if the well be dry!
 This is a goodly place to lie.

1ST BROTHER: My brethren, see—who cometh there
 Slow wending on the hillside bare?

2ND BROTHER: A many-coloured coat I see—
 Our brother, Joseph—yea, 'tis he!

1ST BROTHER: The dreamer cometh! How his dress
 Gleameth in the wilderness! . . .
 Now, hearken, brethren, unto me!
 We are alone, and none may see
 What we shall do beneath the sun,
 And what we do is quickly done.
 Come, let us slay him here, and say
 Some beast hath killed him by the way.

4TH BROTHER *(remaining lying)*:
 Aye, that we shall, and with a will!
 This is a quiet place to kill.

3RD BROTHER: And we shall know, right soon, meseems,
 What will become of all his dreams!

2ND BROTHER: Nay, brethren, do not rashly so,
 Blood turneth not if once it flow.
 But let us choose a way more fit
 And cast him into yonder pit.

5TH BROTHER: Aye, that were better done, till we
    Shall choose what then his fate shall be.

1ST BROTHER: Hush! now he cometh. Hold him fast
    Lest he escape our hands at last.

(Enter Joseph)

JOSEPH: I greet you, brethren. Is it well
    With you —

BRETHREN: With us 'tis very well.
    Hast brought another dream to tell?

JOSEPH: Why look ye so? Why do ye mark
    My words with countenances dark?

3RD BROTHER: We have long marked thy words—too long,
    Till hate hath made our passion strong.
    But since thou comest on this quest
    Thou art indeed our honoured guest,
    And here we have a chamber fit —
    We pray thee, now, to rest in it.

(They seize Joseph)

JOSEPH: God of my fathers, help me now!

(They lower him into the pit)

ALL: What need of heavenly help hast thou
    To whom the stars of heaven bow?

1ST BROTHER: How quick the morning hours have sped!
    I'm hungry. Let us eat some bread.

2ND BROTHER: Some sheep beyond the hill have gone.
    I'll herd them and return anon.—
    Look, yonder comes a dusty train
    Of camel-men across the plain.

(Exit)

1ST BROTHER: From Gilead, with myrrh and spice
    And such-like costly merchandise.
    I wonder if they buy and sell
    Some costlier merchandise as well—
    Brethren—what profit will it be
    To slay our brother secretly
    And spill the blood which is our own?
    He is our flesh, bone of our bone.
    These camel-merchants journey far
    Through all the distant lands that are.
    Come, sell him—let his fortune thus
    Be blamed on heaven and not on us!

3RD BROTHER: Aye, send him forth to foreign lands;
    Let's have no blood upon our hands.

4TH BROTHER: Thou sayest, brother, what is true.
    It is the easiest thing to do.

1ST BROTHER: Then let us hasten, that we may
    Meet with these merchants on their way.

3RD BROTHER: Ho, dreamer, art thou yet awake?
    For now thou must a journey make.

5TH BROTHER: A journey to a country far,
    Beyond the keeping of thy star.

JOSEPH: My brethren, will ye do a deed
    So foul against your father's seed?
    Where's Reuben? He hath loved me best!
    O, tell me it is but a jest!
    Judah—thou wouldst not *sell* me! No—
    Think upon my father's woe—
    And I—thou wouldst not have me leave
    All that I love—no more at eve
    To watch the browsing cattle roam—
    No more to see the tents of home!

1ST BROTHER: Go, take these clinging hands away!
    They learn too tardily to pray.

JOSEPH: Simeon, have mercy—pity me!

3RD BROTHER: 'Tis *thou* that fallest on thy knee
To us thy brethren! Where be now
Thy dreams of stars and sheaves that bow?
'Twere better hadst thou ne'er been born,
Thou pale, unfruitful sheaf of corn!

1ST BROTHER: The merchants come. Go, bid them stay!

4TH BROTHER (*running*): Ho, Sirs, tarry awhile, we pray!

(*Exeunt, dragging Joseph*)

(*Enter 2nd Brother*)

2ND BROTHER: My brethren gone? 'Tis well they be.
Joseph! I'm come to set thee free!

(*Looks into well*)

The lad is not—'tis even so!
And I—whither shall I go?

(*Exit*)

After Scene II

And Joseph was brought down into Egypt, and Potiphar, an officer of Pharoah, Captain of the Guard, an Egyptian, bought him of the hands of the Ishmaelites which had brought him down thither. And the Lord was with Joseph, and he was a prosperous man; and he was in the house of his master, the Egyptian. And the Lord blessed the Egyptian's house for Joseph's sake. And Joseph was a goodly person and well favoured.

And it came to pass after these things that his master's wife tempted Joseph to do evil. But he hearkened not unto her. And when his lord came home she spake unto him saying, The Hebrew servant, which thou hast brought unto us, came in unto me to mock me. And his wrath was kindled, and Joseph's master took him and put him into the prison, a place where the king's prisoners were bound: and he was there in the prison.

And it came to pass that Pharoah dreamed . . . but there was none that could interpret his dream.

SCENE III

Pharoah's Palace

(Pharoah and his Wise Men)

PHAROAH: And are your wells of wisdom dry?
    Your hearts become a desert place?
    Is there no seeing in your eye
    The meaning of a dream to trace?
    Where is great Egypt's secret lore?
    Doth Wisdom walk with us no more?

BUTLER: Now I remember me this day
    When Pharoah's wrath upon me lay
    And on his baker; and we found
    Us both in Pharoah's prison bound.
    Each in one night a dream we dreamed.
    Sore troubled were we, for it seemed
    No man might tell the meaning deep
    That lay within our picture-sleep.
    But now an Hebrew, there in ward,
    Serving the captain of the guard,
    Did mark our sadness, and behold
    The meanings truly did unfold.
    For everything did come to pass
    As his interpretation was.

PHAROAH: Go, hither fetch this fruitful seer,
    And ye, my soothsayers, give ear.
    For wisdom whispers in the wind
    And ye are deaf as ye are blind.
    For now behold a piteous thing,—
    Bereft of wisdom, Egypt's king
    Must search his prison-house to crave
    Counsel from a Hebrew slave!

(Joseph enters)

PHAROAH: Art thou the Hebrew who, 'tis said,

My butler's dream hath truly read?
Couldst thou a dream for me unfold?

JOSEPH: It is no talent that I hold . . .
But God, if so He wills, shall show
What Pharoah's heart doth seek to know.

PHAROAH: I dreamed I by the river stood
Whence seven kine, fat-fleshed and good
Arose and in the meadow fed.
And now from out the river bed
Ascended seven more—but lean,
Ill-favoured, such as ne'er were seen
In all the land. Yet these did eat
The seven fat-fleshed kine for meat,
Nor seemed they, for the feast they had,
The less ill-favoured, lean and bad.
Once more I dreamed, and there appeared
A goodly cornstalk, seven-eared,
And seven others of its kind—
But thin, and withered by the wind,—
Arose within that self-same hour
And did the goodly ears devour.
And I awoke, and now behold
To my magicians I have told
All that I dreamed—but none there be
Who can declare it unto me.

JOSEPH: The dream is one. The seven ears
And seven kine are seven years.
Seven of plenty shall arise
And seven of famine, and the cries
Of man and beast shall mount to heaven.
Forgot shall be the fruitful seven,
The fields lie barren as the sand
And death shall walk through all the land.
God pictureth, as in a glass,
What He shall shortly bring to pass.
Let Pharoah choose a man discreet,
Of wisest heart and willing feet,
And set him over Egypt's land

> To gather corn on every hand
> And store throughout the fruitful years
> The richest of the ripened ears.
> So shall we fear no famine's breath
> And all the land be saved from death.

PHAROAH: Can we find such a one as this,—
> A man in whom God's Spirit is?
> Have we not witnessed, even now,
> That there is none so wise as thou?
> Thy word shall rule throughout the land
> And thou shalt be as my right hand.
> To thee shall all my people bow,
> And none but I more great than thou.

After Scene III

And Joseph went out from the presence of Pharoah and went throughout all the land of Egypt. And in the seven plenteous years the earth brought forth by handfuls. And Joseph gathered corn as the sand of the sea, very much, until he left numbering.

And the seven years of plenteousness were ended, and the famine was over all the face of the earth.

Now when Jacob saw that there was corn in Egypt, Jacob said unto his sons, Why do ye look upon one another? Behold, I have heard that there is corn in Egypt: get you down thither and buy for us from thence; that we may live and not die.

And Joseph's ten brethren went down to buy corn in Egypt. But Benjamin, Joseph's brother, Jacob sent not with his brethren, for he said, Lest peradventure mischief befall him.

SCENE IV

Joseph's Hall of Audience

JOSEPH: Let God be praised, the day is done
> Now doth the fiery-mantled sun
> Sink red upon the burning sand—

And slowly, from the palest star,
The cool night creepeth from afar
To breathe a blessing on the land.
I am a-weary. Let the door
Be shut upon the day. What? More
Await me in the outer hall?
Let them come in—Yet that is all . . .

(*Enter Joseph's brethren. They bow down before Joseph*)

These are the last that I will see.
Now, Sirs, speak, quickly. Who are ye?

BRETHREN: My lord, to purchase corn we come.
The land of Canaan is our home.
Sore is the famine in our land,
But we have silver in our hand;
We pray, my lord, to let us buy,
Lest we and all our cattle die.

JOSEPH (*aside*): (It is my brethren! Long ago
I dreamed this hour,—and it is so.)
Come not before me with your lies!
Ye are no shepherds. Ye are spies!

BRETHREN: My gracious lord, no spies are we!
But one man's sons we truly be.
To buy us food we came, and stand
Ready with . . .

JOSEPH: Ready to spy the land!

JUDAH: Alas, my lord, what shall we do?
Thy servants all are brethren true,—
Twelve sons indeed our father got,
The last is with him—and one—is not.

JOSEPH: Spies are ye all, and now hereby
It shall be proved if ye do lie.
By Pharoah, ye shall go not home
Until your youngest brother come.
Send one of you to fetch him here—
While ye, until it shall appear

        That any truth in you be found,
        Shall lie in prison, locked and bound.

SIMEON: Now are we punished for the sin
        Which we have wrought against our kin.
        Remember how our brother pled
        With bitter words, the tears he shed.
        We saw the anguish of his soul
        And hearkened not.

JUDAH: And now the bowl
        Of bitterness we filled for him
        Is given to us, with flowing brim.

REUBEN: Spake I not unto you that day
        And bade you turn your wrath away?
        But ye were deaf and heedless. Thus
        His blood is now required of us.

JOSEPH (*Turns aside and weeps*):
        If ye be honest men and true,
        And ye would live,—this shall ye do—
        For I fear God . . .
        Let one of you in bonds abide
        While ye in haste shall homeward ride
        With corn for all your house's need;
        But bring to me again with speed
        Your youngest brother, so that I
        May prove you, and ye shall not die.

BRETHREN: My lord, thou are most good and kind!

REUBEN: Now which of us shall stay behind?

JUDAH: 'Tis surely thou—the eldest son!

4TH BROTHER: Nay, it should be the guiltiest one.

5TH BROTHER: We all are guilty. Who is not?

REUBEN: Then it were best to choose by lot.

SIMEON: Choose not at all. Let him remain
        Whose heart doth bear the deepest stain.

Judah did lead us in this thing.
T'was from his breast the thought did spring.
Deny it not ... it was thy boast ...
But I—I hated him the most!
Return ye to your homes and lands ...
Come hither, slave, and bind my hands.

After Scene IV

Then Joseph commanded to fill their sacks with corn and to restore every man's money into his sack and to give them provisions for the way.

And as one of them opened his sack to give his ass provender in the inn, he espied his money; and their hearts failed them, and they were afraid, saying one to another, What is this that God hath done unto us?

And it came to pass, when they had eaten up the corn which they had brought out of Egypt, their father said unto them, Go again, buy us a little food.

And Judah spake unto him saying, The man did solemnly protest unto us saying, Ye shall not see my face except your brother be with you. And their father Israel said unto them, If it must be so now do this: take of the best fruits in the land and carry down the man a present, and take double money in your hand, and the money that was brought again in the mouth of your sacks. Take also your brother, and arise, and God Almighty give you mercy before the man.

SCENE V

JOSEPH'S HOUSE

Enter Brethren with Benjamin (and slave)

REUBEN: I fear this man. Why are we brought
    Into his house?

JUDAH: It is a plot
    To seize us all for slaves, and say
    We tried to steal his corn away.

4TH BROTHER: Our money hidden in the sack!

5TH BROTHER: His zeal to bring us quickly back!

REUBEN: How cunningly his plans are set!

JUDAH: We're caught like sparrows in a net!

(Enter Joseph)

JOSEPH: Ah, Sirs, I bid you welcome! Say,
    Doth peace dwell in your hearts alway?
    How doth the old man—your father—thrive?
    Is he well and yet alive?

BRETHREN *(bowing)*: Our father is alive and well.

JOSEPH: And is this he of whom ye tell—
    Your brother, and the youngest one?
    May God be good to thee, my son!

(Turns and weeps)

    My friends, I welcome you, and pray
    That ye will dine with me this day.
    Your brother, now from prison freed,
    Will eat with us, and comes with speed.

BRETHREN *(whispering)*: What meaneth he by this request?
    Shall slaves become their master's guest?

JOSEPH: The feast in yonder room is spread.
    Ho, ye, within there! Set on bread!

(Exeunt)

During Scene V

And Joseph commanded the steward of his house saying, Fill the men's sacks with food, as much as they can carry, and put every man's money in his sack's mouth. And put my cup, the silver cup, in the sack's mouth of the youngest.

And when they were gone out of the city, and not yet far off, Joseph said unto his steward, Up, follow after the men and say unto them, Wherefore have ye rewarded evil for good? Is not this the cup in which my Lord drinketh and whereby indeed he divineth? Ye have done evil in so doing.

And the cup was found in Benjamin's sack, and they rent their clothes and laded every man his ass, and returned to the city.

Scene V (continued)

BRETHREN (*off*): (1) Wherefore should we steal this thing?
           (2) Double money did we bring!
           (3) And a present in our hand—
           (4) Choicest fruits of Canaan's land.
           (5) And the silver in our sack
           (6) We did bring it safely back!

(*Enter Brethren* (*speaking*) (*after each one has said his line, they continue with their lines, all talking at once*))

(*Enter Joseph*)

JOSEPH: What deed is this that ye have done?
    Is this the thanks that I have won?
    Do ye thus for kindness pay?

BRETHREN: Alas, my lord, what shall we say
    To clear ourselves of this offence?
    How can we prove our innocence?
    God saw our sinfulness of yore—
    We are thy slaves for evermore.

JOSEPH: Nay, God forbid. Let him be bound
    With whom the silver cup was found.
    And ye—may your afflictions cease—
    And to your father—go in peace.

JUDAH: My lord, let now thy servant near
    To speak a word within thine ear.
    Let not thy wrath against me burn,
    Nor coldly from my prayer turn. . . .
    Our father loves the lad—and said:
    "His brother, whom I loved, is dead.
    "Ye shall not take the little one
    "Lest I should lose my youngest son.

"For if mischance befall him, I
"With sorrowing shall surely die."
And to my father I did swear
The boy should never leave my care,
And if mischance upon him came
That I should ever bear the blame.
Now let me in his place abide
A bondman to my lord, and hide
My face for ever, lest thy slave
Should send his father to the grave.

JOSEPH (*weeps*): Come nearer unto me, I pray.
I am he ye sold away—
Joseph! Doth my father live? . . .
I am Joseph . . . let it give
No trouble to your hearts to know
That God the Lord hath willed it so.
For God did send me forth to make
A dwelling for your children's sake,
Prepare a place where ye might bide
Through all the deathly famine-tide.
For, yet five barren years remain
Wherein shall grow not stalk nor grain.
So to my father haste and say:
"Thus saith Joseph, thy son, this day:
" 'God hath made me Egypt's lord.
Come down, I pray, with one accord
Thou and thy flocks and all thy seed
And I will nourish thee and feed
Thy children's children in the land
Which I will give thee from my hand' " . . .

BRETHREN: 'Tis true, 'tis true—'tis surely he!
What can we do, or whither flee?

JOSEPH: Come, tremble not, for ye shall live.
It was God's will, and I forgive.

BRETHREN (*kneeling*): My lord—our brother—let us now
In thankfulness before thee bow.
We are not worthy of thy grace . . .

JOSEPH: Now, let me see my father's face—
Arise, make all the haste ye may—
And quarrel not upon your way!

Reading after Scene V

And Joseph placed his father and his brethren and gave them a possession in the land of Egypt, in the best of the land, as Pharoah commanded.

And Joseph nourished his father and his brethren, and all his father's household.

And Israel dwelt in the land of Egypt, and they had possessions therein, and grew and multiplied exceedingly.

THE LAST PLAGUE

(age 8–9)

This, the story of the Exodus, is a simpler play than the previous one. Again, of course, the children should know the whole background before attempting it. Much depends here on the choruses; and at the end, the Israelitish woman pitying the stricken Egyptian, while the marching song of triumph is heard dying away in the distance, can make a very moving curtain.

> SCENE: *The house of a family of Israelites in Egypt during the oppression. Some women are grouped round a bed on which lies a youth. A group of men stand near the door.*

CHORUS OF WOMEN:
> Woe unto us, our hope is fled!
> Woe to the bearers of Pharaoh's yoke!
> With fruits of bitterness are we fed,
> For surely the Lord hath forsaken his folk.

CHORUS OF MEN:
> For Moses hath lifted his rod on high,
> And the waters of Egypt were red with blood,
> And hail and lightning from the sky
> Wasted the fields and the blossoms in bud.

CHORUS OF WOMEN:
> But yet the more grievous was Pharaoh's yoke,
> For surely the Lord hath forsaken his folk.

CHORUS OF MEN:
> Now loathsome frogs in the cities sprawl,
> The cattle are stricken, and, countless as sand,
> Flies are blackening house and hall,
> And locusts devouring the fair green land.

CHORUS OF WOMEN:
> But yet the more grievous was Pharoah's yoke,
> For surely the Lord hath forsaken his folk.

(Enter an Egyptian taskmaster)

EGYPTIAN: Ho! idle son of an idle race,
    Why hidest thou thy craven face?

MOTHER: The lad is my son. Thou speakest in vain,
    For low he lies on a bed of pain,
    Nigh unto death with lashes sore.
    How can he labour for Pharaoh more?

EGYPTIAN: With mine own hand these strokes I gave,
    For he is a slothful, idle slave.
    Full fifty short was his tale of brick....

MOTHER: Hold back, Egyptian, wouldst strike at the sick?
    Behold how his flesh with thy whip is raw!
    How should he make brick if thou give him no straw?

EGYPTIAN: Let him arise at the dawn of the day
    To gather the straw, to dig for the clay.
    Better to perish 'neath Pharaoh's yoke
    Than softly to die among womenfolk.

MOTHER: Hast thou no heart, O pitiless one?
    Has thou thyself no firstborn son?

EGYPTIAN: Never for slaves shall my heart be torn.
    I too have a son; but he is *free*-born.

(Exit Egyptian)

(Enter Messenger)

MESSENGER: Thus saith Moses: "Thus saith the Lord:
    This night through Egypt shall I pass.
    Hearken, O Israel, to my word,
    Lest ye be trodden as the grass.
    Take, every house, a spotless lamb,
    And paint with blood upon the door
    A sign which showeth that I am
    Thy Lord. So shall I pass thee o'er.
    For at the midnight hour I go
    To smite the first-born of the land,
    And there shall arise a cry of woe,
    A grievous cry on every hand,
    As ne'er in Egypt hath been known,

A cry from the captive, a cry from the throne.
But ye shall eat in haste, and bide
Ready, with staff, and girdle bound,
To make a journey, to march, to ride,—
And none to hinder you shall be found.
For ye shall go forth with a mighty hand,
To the home of our fathers—the promised land.
Thus saith the Lord."

(Exit)

CHORUS OF MEN AND WOMEN:
Now let all Israel rejoice,
For the Lord hath remembered his people.
For the word of the Lord is gone forth,
As thunder it shaketh the proud.
For the servants of Pharaoh shall quail,
And the chariots of Egypt shall tremble,
In the day of the might of the Lord,
In the day of the triumph of Israel.
O ye daughters of Israel, rejoice!
Let the sons of our fathers arise!
For the day of our darkness is past,
And the morning of triumph is nigh.
Now let all Israel rejoice!
For the Lord hath remembered his people.

(During the last words, all go out except the group of women, and the stage is in darkness.)

A VOICE: And it came to pass, that at midnight the Lord smote all the first-born in the land of Egypt, from the first-born of Pharaoh that sat on his throne unto the first-born of the captive that was in the dungeon; and all the first-born of cattle.

And Pharaoh rose up in the night, he and all his servants, and all the Egyptians; and there was a great cry in Egypt; for there was not a house where there was not one dead.

(During the last words cries are heard, and as the lights go up:
Woe, alas, my son is dead,
Woe unto Egypt, doom and woe!)

(Enter Egyptian taskmaster)

EGYPTIAN: Go, go from this place—'tis Pharaoh's command!
　　Take your children, your cattle, up, out of this land!
　　Go, worship your God,—that His will may be done!
　　He hath stricken our folk,—He hath smitten my son!

(He sinks down on his knees)

(Enter a woman. She speaks in ecstasy)

WOMAN: Hear ye the sound of the marching of thousands,
　　Under the stars to the land of the sun?
　　Hark how the feet of the sons of Jehovah
　　Trample the dust of the days that are done!
　　Shake thou the earth with a sound as of thunder,
　　Onward, O Israel, thy day is begun!

(The group rises, and the other Israelites pass across the stage, carrying bundles, young people, old folk bent and hobbling, and children—loitering. Four men lift the bed and follow out. Only the mother is left. She turns to the Egyptian)

MOTHER: *Thy* son—not mine—it had to be.
　　The God of Israel pity thee.

(Exit Mother. The Egyptian falls to the ground. The chorus of marching Israelites is heard, growing fainter)

CHORUS: Now let all Israel rejoice
　　For the Lord hath remembered His people.
　　For the word of the Lord is gone forth,
　　As thunder it shaketh the proud. . . .

SLOW CURTAIN

SAUL

(age 8–9)

The subject of this play is of course the tragedy of Saul's disobedience—a very good theme for children just at this age! It is more suitable for nine-year-olds, depending chiefly on individual parts—Saul, Samuel, Jonathan, the Witch of Endor—while the chorus is less in evidence. The story itself is in keeping with the more pronounced individuality belonging to age 9, of which many teachers of nine-year-olds will be aware, as compared with the "softer" nature of the eight-year-old for whom the stories of Joseph and the Last Plague are more suited. This play, in short, demands some individual acting. The primitive emotions of jealousy, rage, fear and righteous anger can well be evoked by the children, and much can be made of the several dramatic moments. In the Endor scene it is preferable that the spirit of Samuel should not remain merely a voice, but that he should be seen to rise slowly from behind some object and to sink again with his last words.

SCENE I

CHORUS: Samuel was old and full of days,
　　　　His children walked not in his ways.
　　　　"Give us a king!" the people cried
　　　　"To lead us forth in battle's pride,
　　　　To judge and rule us, and to be
　　　　The light of Israel's majesty."

SAMUEL: Thus saith the Lord: "This people's will
　　　　Shall bring them woe, shall bring them ill.
　　　　To earthly vanities they cling.
　　　　They have forsaken Me, their King.
　　　　Yet hearken to their voice, and show
　　　　What manner of king shall reign below."
　　　　Your children he will take for gain
　　　　To wage his wars, to reap his grain.
　　　　Your sheep, your vines, your corn, your seed
　　　　He will take freely for his need.
　　　　Then shall ye sore bewail your lot
　　　　And God the Lord will hearken not.

CHORUS: Nevertheless, we crave this thing:
   Make unto us a king, a king!

SAMUEL: Go—thrust your fingers in the fire!
   The Lord will grant you your desire.

SCENE II

Saul Returning from Battle

(Throne left. Half open curtains back, through which Saul enters)

CHORUS: Hail, O Saul, whose arm of might
   Hath brought us glory in the fight!
   Of thee shall every nation tell.
   Hail, thou king of Israel!

SAUL: Hear, princes, elders, people all—
   Thus did the battle fierce befall—
   The Lord our God did me command
   To smite the Amalekite, foot and hand.
   This have I done, for Israel's sword
   Was urged and strengthened by the Lord.

   (Moves to throne)

CHORUS: Hail, king and ruler, thou shalt be
   The light of Israel's majesty!

SAUL: This is my purpose—wisely and well
   To rule my people Israel.
   Therefore take heed that ye obey
   The law of God the Lord alway.
   Bow ye not down to stick or stone,
   But worship God the Lord alone.
   From this day forth I make decree
   No witchcraft in the land shall be,
   But such as deal in magic lore
   Shall die—that witches be no more.

So let us ever serve the Lord
With hearts attentive to His word.

(Sits)

CHORUS: We hearken, and we haste, O king,
To do thy will in everything.

(Retire)

(Enter Samuel. Saul descends to meet him)

SAUL: Blessed be thou, O man of God,
Upon His enemies have I trod
And have performed the Lord's command.

SAMUEL: What meaneth then, on every hand,
The bleating of the sheep I hear,
Lowing of oxen in mine ear?

SAUL: From the Amalekites they come.
Of flocks and herds we gathered some—
Of all the sheep and kine the best—
But utterly destroyed the rest.
These have the people spared the sword
To sacrifice them to the Lord.

SAMUEL: When thou wast little in thy sight
Wast thou not made a man of might,
Anointed king of all thy race?
Why has thou turned aside thy face
From the commandment of the Lord
And taken spoil for thy reward?

SAUL: His voice I surely have obeyed,
In naught from his commandment strayed,
Utterly to destroy and smite
The sinner, the Amalekite.
The people certain spoils did bring
To make a burnt offering.

SAMUEL: Thinkest thou that the Lord thy God
Before whose face our fathers trod,
Doth more in offerings rejoice

> Than in obedience to His voice?
> Behold, to hearken and obey
> Is more than fat of rams, and they
> That love rebellion take their part
> With idols and the witches' art.
> Thus hath spoken God the Lord:
> Because thou didst reject His word
> Rejected thou shalt also be
> From all thy kingly majesty.

(Samuel turns to go, and Saul lays hold upon his cloak, which is rent)

SAMUEL: Thus hath the Lord from thee this day
    Thy kingdom, Israel, torn away,
    And straightway shall anoint the brow
    Of one full worthier than thou.

SAUL: Stay! I have sinned! Yet with me stay
    And still before my folk, I pray
    Show honour to me as of yore—
    And worship God with me, once more.

(Samuel turns, and they worship)

SCENE III

Saul on His Throne

CHORUS: Now gone is Samuel from the king,
    And gone his gracious counselling.
    So sitteth Saul on a fruitless throne,
    Unloved, unsought, unblessed, alone.
    While, through the hours of horror dim
    An evil spirit troubleth him.

SAUL *(fiercely)*: Go—fetch me Jonathan, my son—
    And leave our presence—everyone!

(Exeunt Chorus)

Ah—how shall I fill the empty days

Bereft of God—the people's praise
No longer music in mine ears—
Distraught by envy, hates and fears?
I am resolved a deed to do

(*Enter Jonathan*)

To bring me peace of heart. Thou too
Shalt aid me, Jonathan. Come hither
And let us now commune together.
My son, thou knowest how this throne—
Inheritance for thee alone—
Shall pass from me unto another,
To him—thy much-loved foster-brother.
Aye, well I know thou dost extol
This son of Jesse—that thy soul
Is knit with his, I know not why—
Yet surely shall this David die!

JONATHAN: Why should he die? Let not the king
Seek to do this wicked thing.
Behold, how faithful he hath been
To thee-ward, nor have any seen
One more valiant in the fight.
Did he not great Goliath smite?
And put his life into his hand
The mighty giant to withstand?
As Captain of thy battle-line
How oft he o'ercame the Philistine!
Didst thou not see it, and rejoice?
My father, hearken to my voice,
'Gainst thee hath David done no wrong.

SAUL: Nay—but I heard the victory song
The women sang when on a day
We homeward journeyed from the fray:
In every city was it sung,
And hath my heart with anguish wrung:
"Saul hath slain his thousands and David his tens of thousands".
"Saul hath slain his thousands and David his tens of thousands."
Of him ten thousands did they sing

Of me, but thousands. So the king
Was deemed to be of less renown!
What lacks he now but Israel's crown?

JONATHAN: Yet David hath most meekly borne
The people's praises, and hath worn
His honours as a mantle spread,
A garment lightly to be shed.
Behold, he loves thee, this I know,
And doth before the people show
His reverence for thee. Shall our laws
Slay a man without a cause?

SAUL: I have hearkened—have no care.
As the Lord liveth, here I swear
That I shall seek no more to slay. . . .
Bring him hither, that he play
Sweet music to me, and console
With harmony my bruiséd soul.

(*Exit Jonathan. Enter David*)

DAVID: Thy servant waits: What wills the king?

SAUL: I beg of thee thy harp to string
And, as aforetime thou didst play,
With music charm my thoughts away.

(*David begins to play. From without, the women sing:* "Saul has slain his thousands", *etc. Saul seizes his javelin and throws it, shouting*)
Die, thou slave!

(*David escapes*)

SCENE IV

(*before traverse curtain*)

GILBOA: ON THE BATTLEFIELD

SAUL: The Philistines have brought their hosts.
Like locusts border they our coasts.

Of counsel I am sore in need.
The Lord doth answer not, nor heed
My bitter prayer. Samuel is dead,
And David to the enemy fled.
Whom shall we find in wisdom rich?
Seek me a woman who is a witch!

1ST OFFICER: A witch? Did not my Lord decree
That none such in the land should be?
Where should I seek for such an one?

SAUL: Go—anywhere beneath the sun!

2ND OFFICER: My lord—but let the king forgive—
I know where such an one doth live—
At Endor—in a lonely place—

SAUL: Then let us journey there apace

(*Exeunt Officers*)

This night the future I must know
And where our faltering feet should go.

SCENE V

ENDOR

(*A cauldron on a fire, left. The witch crouching over it stirring. A loud knock at the door. The witch frightened, goes slowly to the door. Enter Saul and two officers*)

WITCH: What seek ye at this midnight hour?

SAUL: Call up, I pray thee, by thy power
The soul of him whom I shall name.

WITCH: What! Would ye then that I proclaim
Myself a witch? Hath not King Saul
Cast out wizards, witches all?
Wherefore come ye here to pry
And set a snare, that I may die?

SAUL: As the Lord liveth, I set no snare,
   No harm shall come to thee, I swear.

WITCH: Whom, then, seek ye? Swiftly tell.

SAUL: Bring up the soul of Samuel.

(*The witch stands over the cauldron, her back to Saul. Suddenly, she swings round*)

WITCH: Thou hast deceived me—thou art Saul!

SAUL: Peace, woman, nothing shall befall
   But I shall keep thy secret still.
   Fear not, but only do my will.
   What sawest thou?

WITCH: I see him rise
   An old man, mantle-wrapped, his eyes
   Do pierce my soul with flames of fire . . .

VOICE OF SAMUEL: Wherefore hast thou with base desire
   Disquieted my spirit's rest?

SAUL (*kneeling*): I am afraid and sore distressed.
   The Philistines oppress me sore.
   God is departed, and no more
   Doth answer my most anxious prayer.
   Thus have I called thee, that thou share
   Thy wisdom with me. Do thou say
   What I shall do this day.

SAMUEL: Wherefore dost thou ask of me,
   Since God is now thine enemy?
   Thy kingdom from thee now is riven
   And to thy neighbour, David, given.
   Because thou didst not God obey
   This thing is done to thee this day;
   The host of Israel, thou and thine
   Delivered to the Philistine. . . .
   And, from thine earthly dwelling free,
   Tomorrow shalt thou be with me.

TABLEAU

(*Saul and his armour-bearer lie dead on Mount Gilboa. Israelites approach*)

CHORUS: How are the mighty fallen!
Tell it not in Gath,
Publish it not in the streets of Askelon,
Lest the daughters of the Philistines rejoice,
Lest the daughters of the Gentiles triumph.
Ye mountains of Gilboa,
Let there be no dew, neither let there be rain upon you, nor fields of offerings;
For there the shield of the mighty is vilely cast away,
The shield of Saul, as though he had not been anointed with oil.
How are the mighty fallen,
And the weapons of war perished.

CURTAIN

CHRISTMAS PLAY

(age 8–9)

This Christmas Play is a little unusual in that it has its beginnings in the Garden of Eden. The Christmas event, after all, derives its significance from the existence of evil in the world, and the three short scenes which precede the Christmas Play proper show the steps which led to that event.

Those adults who still tend to shrink from teaching young children the story of Adam and Eve because it is not considered "scientific", should bear in mind that events can be expressed pictorially as well as intellectually; and young children, having a natural affinity with all that is pictorial, should be allowed to live in their imagination and such stories are therefore eminently suited to them.

THE GARDEN OF EDEN

Adam, Eve, and the serpent (hidden)

CHORUS: When God made man of earthly dust
    And breathed in him the breath of life,
    A garden fair he gave in trust
    To Adam the man and to Eve his wife.
    And there God planted every tree
    To give them joy, to yield them food,
    The Tree of Life in the midst set He,
    And the Tree of Knowledge of Evil and Good.
    Now God commanded the man: Thou mayst
    Eat of all fruits which please thine eye,
    But the Tree of Knowledge thou shalt not taste,
    For in that day thou shalt surely die.
    Now the subtlest beast which God had made—
    The supple serpent—raised his head. . . .

SERPENT: Hath God the Lord commanded thee
    Thou shouldst not eat of any tree?

EVE: God gave us every herb for meat
    Save one, of which we may not eat—

The Tree of Knowledge, from whose root
   Death flows to every leaf and fruit.

SERPENT: Nay, 'tis not so! Ye shall not die.
   In that same fruit doth wisdom lie.
   God knoweth, when ye taste that tree,
   Your eyes will open, ye shall see!
   Then shall ye be like God, and know
   Both good and evil here below.
   Awake thy sight and ope thine eyes,
   Come, taste the fruit, and be thou wise!

EVE: The fruit hangs golden on the tree,
   Sweet to the taste and fair to see,
   And if not death but wisdom flow
   In that soft flesh, and I shall know
   The hidden things of earth and skies—
   Come, gentle fruit, and make me wise!

(She plucks the fruit and eats)

   Adam, awaken from thy dream!
   Taste of this fruit! The world doth seem
   Filled with new wonders, deep and broad . . .

(Adam eats also)

ADAM: O, let me hide myself from God!

CHORUS: Adam, where art thou?

ADAM: Here am I.
   I heard thy voice, and I did fly,
   Afraid to see Thee face to face,
   For naked stand we in this place.

CHORUS: Who told thee thou wast so? Hast thou
   Eaten the forbidden bough?

ADAM: The woman whom Thou gavest me
   Did pluck the fruit from off the tree,
   And I did eat.

EVE: The serpent came the leaves among
   And tempted me with guileful tongue,
   And I did eat.

CHORUS: For that he tempted man the first
   Above all cattle shall he be cursed,
   Dust shall he eat, and all his days
   Mankind shall be his enemies.
   For thee, O man, this fate is found—
   Cursed for thy sake shall be the ground,
   Thorns and thistles it now shall bear,
   In the sweat of thy brow shalt thou labour there;
   Sorrow and pain ye both shall know
   To sickness and death your ways shall go
   Until at last to the ground ye turn,
   For dust thou art and to dust return.
   And, behold, lest now ye should,
   Knowing the evil and the good,
   Stretch forth your hands to the Tree of Life,
   And live for ever—thou and thy wife
   Forth from the garden ye shall be thrust,
   Into the darkness, into the dust.

(Enter Angel)

   And now the angel of God shall stand
   To guard the gate of the heavenly land
   With the flame of a sword that shall gather to strife,
   To keep the way of the Tree of Life.

ADAM: Is there no hope our feet may pass
   Once more o'er heaven's dewy grass?

ANGEL: Thy feet shall know a harder way.
   Far must thou fare, O man, nor stay
   Lingering thus at heaven's gate,
   But follow thy downward path of fate.
   Behold the sin which ye began
   Liveth and groweth, O woman and man!

CAIN AND ABEL

(Adam and Eve watch the scene which follows)

CHORUS: Behold now Adam's eldest son
    Goes forth at eve, his labour done,
    And bears as offering to God,
    The fruits of the ground, of the earthly sod.
    Abel his brother has come from the field
    The firstlings of his flock to yield,
    And each now builds an altar high,
    Under the gold of the evening sky.

ABEL: The smoke of mine offering mounteth to heaven.
    Thanks be to God who all things hath given.

CAIN: Mine altar's smoke doth downward drift.
    The Lord accepteth not my gift.

CHORUS: Why is thy face cast down, O Cain?
    Thine offering shall not be in vain
    If thou doest well—and if thou fail,
    No sacrifices shall avail.

CAIN: Thou wretched shepherd, idle clod!
    Thinkest thou thus to please thy God?
    I'll see no sacrifice of thine
    Flaming upwards over mine.
    Henceforth in my *strength* shall *my* glory be.
    And I'll make a sacrifice of *thee*!

(Strikes him, and Abel falls dead)

CHORUS: Cain, Cain, where is thy brother?

CAIN: Am I the keeper of another?
    I know not.

CHORUS: Yet the voice doth sound
    Of blood which crieth from the ground.
    Cursed by the earth now shalt thou be.
    Its strength it shall not yield to thee,

> But shunned by all men shalt thou live,
> A wanderer and a fugitive.

EVE: Is there no hope, O shining one,
> To soothe the sorrows of my son?

ANGEL: From me O learn to turn thy face
> And seek the light in an earthly place.
> Behold, a man of God shall stand
> Obedient to his Lord's command,
> And from his faithfulness shall spring
> The promise of a heavenly King.

ABRAHAM AND ISAAC

(Adam and Eve still watching)

CHORUS: Abraham, Abraham, take thy son,
> Thine only son whom thou dost love,
> To the land of Moriah, unto one
> Of the mountains I will tell thee of.
> And thither thou the lad shalt bring
> To be a burnt offering.

(Enter Abraham, Isaac and servants)

ABRAHAM: Now is our journey all but done,
> For thrice the fiery-mantled sun
> Hath lit his path across the skies. . . .
> And yonder now the mountain lies. . . .
> Abide ye with the ass, until
> The lad and I on yonder hill
> Shall worship God the Lord, and then
> Return to you again.

ISAAC: Father, my father . . .

ABRAHAM: Here I am . . .

ISAAC: I have the wood and thou the fire,
> But where, my father, is the lamb

To do the Lord's desire?
How shall our sacrifice be done?

ABRAHAM: God will provide a lamb, my son.

(*They proceed on their journey. Abraham binds Isaac and lays him on the altar. He is about to slay him*)

CHORUS: Abraham! Abraham!

ABRAHAM: Here am I.

CHORUS: Touch not the lad, nor let him die
A sacrifice upon the stone,
For God careth for His own.
But now because thou hadst not spared
Thine only son and wast prepared
To offer him unto the Lord,
God knoweth thou dost fear His word.

ISAAC: See father, yonder is a ram
Caught in the thicket by the horn . . .

ABRAHAM: Thus doth the Lord provide the lamb.
Come, let us take him from the thorn
And let our sacrifice be done
In thanksgiving for thee, my son.

CHORUS: Thus saith the Lord thy God on high:
Because thy son thou wouldst have given,
Thy children I shall multiply
In number like the stars of heaven.
Yea, I will make them as the sand
That lieth at the ocean's breast;
And in thy seed shall every land
Through all the earth be blessed.

JOSEPH AND MARY

CHORUS: There come two weary travellers
Along a wintry road.
They have no shelter from the blast,

> No welcoming abode.
> But on they journey to the town
> Wherein they hope to find
> Some humble inn to shelter them
> And shield them from the wind.

JOSEPH: I pray thee, sir, hast thou a bed
> Whereon my wife might lay her head?
> Far have we travelled since the day
> And we are weary of the way.

1ST INNKEEPER: Beds? I've no beds! The house is full.
> There's not a bench, there's not a stool
> Whereon a cat might find a space.
> Go, seek ye in some other place!

JOSEPH (*to 2nd Innkeeper*):
> A little shelter, sir, I pray
> Until the dawning of the day.

2ND INNKEEPER: I have no room for such as ye;
> This is a rich man's hostelry.
> I'll have no beggars at my door.
> Be off, and trouble me no more!

JOSEPH (*to 3rd Innkeeper*): O sir, my prayer I fear to speak—
> The humblest lodging do we seek.

3RD INNKEEPER: Alas, I have not the humblest kind—
> But if perchance ye both be able
> To take some comfort from a stable—
> Ye shall be sheltered from the wind.
> Come, let me lead you to the door.
> Welcome ye are to its rugged floor.

A HILLSIDE

(*Three shepherds lie down to sleep*)

CHORUS: Long ago on this night so still
> Three shepherds lay down on a lonely hill.

The stars shone clear in a silver sky,
And the white frost glistened in cold reply.
The pale light shadowed the silent sheep,
And wrapped the earth in a veil of sleep.
Then suddenly out of the dark there swings
The sound of singing, the flash of wings,
And angels of God make bright as day
The lonesome fields and the mountains grey.
They sing of a child whose wondrous birth
Brings joy and peace to the men of earth.

(*The children sing: "First Nowell" v.1.*)

(*Enter Angel*)

ANGEL: Fear not, for tidings now I bring
Of Him who is born to be your King,
And ye shall find Him, if ye go
To Bethlehem, in a manger low.
Glory to God in highest heaven,
Peace on the earth to men be given.

1ST SHEPHERD: My brothers, I am sore amazed!
Surely should the Lord be praised!

2ND SHEPHERD: Then shall we not at once away
To Bethlehem, ere the break of day?

3RD SHEPHERD: What presents could we take of worth
To Him, the Lord of heaven and earth?

1ST SHEPHERD: Fear not, the gift that he will prize
From our own labours shall arise.

2ND SHEPHERD: Some wool will serve to keep Him warm,
And save Him from the winter's harm.

3RD SHEPHERD: Some milk I'll take, that He be fed,
Some butter, meal and softest bread.

1ST SHEPHERD: And I a lamb will gladly bring
As offering to the baby King.

(*Joseph, and Mary holding Baby, seated in the background*)
(*Children sing "Joseph dearest"; "O Little Town of Bethlehem"*)

SHEPHERDS: "How far is it to Bethlehem?

CHORUS: Not very far.

SHEPHERDS: Shall we find the stable-room
  Lit by a star?
  Can we see the little child,
  Is he within?
  If we lift the wooden latch,
  May we go in?"*

   (*Shepherds now approach Joseph and Mary*)

3RD SHEPHERD: I come, Lord Jesus, thee to greet,
  With simple foods as shepherds eat.

2ND SHEPHERD: And I, hoping thou wilt bless—
  Some wool to shield Thy nakedness.

1ST SHEPHERD: And I, unworthy as I am,
  Have brought, O King, a snow-white lamb.

MARY: Shepherds, your gifts I gladly take
  Of warmth and comfort, for His sake.
  May angels bless you from above
  And God reward you for your love.

   (*Children sing "O Come All Ye Faithful", while the three innkeepers, Abraham and Isaac, Cain and Abel, Adam and Eve, the Angel and the serpent, approach and kneel*)

   * From *Oxford Book of Carols*. This could be sung.

THE DEATH OF BALDUR

(age 9–10)

This is the well-known story from the Norse Legends. The farther back we go in the history of ancient peoples, the more we enter the era of Myth and Legend, and from these tales we see that men in those days were much more concerned and familiar with a spiritual world than they were to become later, and we can trace a gradual "descent" from this state of human religious experience towards the almost godless outlook of the later Roman period. But with this loss of the old religious outlook there developed a new human capacity, that of intellectual thought which began most noticeably with the philosophers of Greece and led at length to our modern science.

The legend of Baldur can be regarded as a picture of the approaching "death" of the old natural religions with the dimming of the sense of a spiritual world—the twilight of the gods. Evolution could not be stayed, and the old dreamy consciousness, last traces of which are sometimes still seen in Celtic peoples even today, had to give way to the clarity of thinking. So, in this story, despite every effort to stem this trend of religious darkening (illumined in a new way with the advent of Christianity), Baldur, the god of light, is lost. But there is a hint in the old legend that it is not for ever.

It is a beautiful story, with joy suddenly turned to pathos as the body of Baldur, to the accompaniment of a solemn dirge, is slowly borne to the funeral ship which is to be set alight and sent out to sea, in the manner of the Norsemen. Then follows Hermod's dramatic ride to the realm of the dead, and the tragedy of his almost successful venture turning to failure in the end.

SCENE I

Asgard

(Enter Odin, R., Baldur, followed by Gods, L.)

CHORUS OF GODS: Baldur the Beautiful, god of light,
 Robed in the sunshine, peerless, bright,
 Pure of brow as the lily white,
 Gladden our hearts with thy golden light!

ODIN: Why walks my son in woeful wise,
With heedless foot and troubled eyes?
Our days are dark, our joy is done
When clouded is thy face, my son.

CHORUS: Baldur the Beautiful, etc.

BALDUR: All-father Odin, wise thou art
To see the shadow in my heart.
I grieve, my father, for the day
When Fate shall take my life away
And pale among the dead I stand
In Hela's dim unlighted land.

CHORUS: Shall Baldur die? Shall light no more
Shine upon the Asgard shore?

BALDUR: I dreamed a cloud rose, darkly spun,
And hid all Asgard from the sun.
Again I dreamed, and withered, grey,
The trees and flowers lifeless lay,
While darkness spread her dismal wing,
And all the gods sat sorrowing.
Yet once again I dreamed, and lo,
A voice in darkness, crying "Woe",
"A feast in Hela's realm is spread,"
"For Baldur the Beautiful is dead."

CHORUS: Woe unto us when light is sped,
And Baldur the Beautiful—lies dead!

FRIGGA: This shall not be. Let counsel wise
Gently in our hearts arise,
And seek how safety may be won
For Baldur, my beloved son.

THOR: Who dares hurt Baldur? Let him stand
In heaven or earth, on sea or land,
And I, with Miölnir in my hand. . . .

HODER: More strong than wise, O hasty Thor!
Will he make known his deed before?

Else will thy succour come too late
To save our brother from his fate.

ODIN: Blind thou art, Hoder, yet hast sight
Illumined by an inner light!

FRIGGA: Hear my counsel! Let us hie
Through all the earth and sea and sky
And beg of each created thing
That it no harm to Baldur bring.
A solemn oath shall swear to me
Both bird and beast, and stone and tree,
Earth and water, fire and air,
Iron, bronze and metals rare,
Venom of the serpent's tooth,
And diseases void of ruth.
Fire shall promise, steel shall pledge
That neither flame nor weapon's edge
Shall mar the whiteness of his skin,
Nor let the bane of sorrow in.

CHORUS (*separately*): O bird, O beast,
O stone, O tree,
Wilt thou promise solemnly?
O earth, O water,
Fire and air,
Iron, bronze,
And metals rare,
Venom of the serpent's tooth,
And diseases void of ruth?

CHORUS (*all*): Fire, O promise, steel, O pledge
That neither flame nor weapon's edge
Shall mar the whiteness of his skin,
Nor let the bane of sorrow in.

(*Exeunt*)

(*Loki enters, and peers malevolently after them. Exit, mimicking them*)

SCENE II

(Frigga, seated, spinning. Hoder standing apart)
(Shouting, off. Enter Thor, excited)
(Laughter)

THOR (*pointing off*):
    See Baldur, smiling in a ring
    Of gods and weapons! Not one thing
    We hurl at him can bring him harm.

(Exit)

FRIGGA: My son is safe. There is a charm
    About his life, which none may break. . . .

(Laughter)

    Hark, Hoder, at the mirth they make!

HODER: I hear, but see not. Would I were
    With them, to make it merrier!

(Enter Loki, disguised as an old woman)

LOKI: Good day, fair dame!

FRIGGA: Good day to you!
    Know you what the Aesir do?

LOKI: Right well! The Aesir in a ring
    Stones and spears at Baldur fling,
    Hew with axe and strike with sword,
    And yet no hurt to him accord.

FRIGGA: 'Tis true! No weapon, tree or stone
    Will injure Baldur. He alone
    Is safe, whatever may befall,
    For I have taken oaths of all.

LOKI: Have *all* things given oaths to thee?

FRIGGA: West of Valhalla grows a tree
    And on its branch a tiny shoot—
    A tender plant without a root;

THE DEATH OF BALDUR

Too weak upon the earth to grow,
Thus gently clings the mistletoe.
So young it seemed, that I was loth
To ask of it a solemn oath.

LOKI: The mistletoe! Too young, no doubt.
What harm could come of such a sprout?

(Laughter) (Exit)

HODER: How fares my brother? Goes it well?
I fear for him . . . I cannot tell . . .
Should some mischance befall him now . . .

FRIGGA: Upright he stands, and calm of brow,
With smiling lips and laughing eye,
While round him scatheless weapons lie.
How glorious and bright his face,
Baldur, the splendour of our race.

HODER: If only I had eyes to see
His glory, I should happy be . . .

(Enter Loki)

FRIGGA: Ah, Loki, dost thou join the band?
Hast brought a weapon in thy hand?

LOKI *(hiding it behind his back)*: Only a tiny thing—a jest . . .
Good Hoder,—dost not join the rest?
Why standest thou with face of woe?

HODER: Alas, I have no spear to throw,
Nor can I tell where Baldur stands
And whither I should point my hands.

LOKI: Come, let me help thee,—there the place,—
'Tis distant but a little space—
And here a weapon—grasp it so—
A twig that did but lately grow
Upon a nearby tree—a dart
That needs but little throwing art.

(Laughter)

My hand shall guide thee,—gently, so—
There standeth Baldur—quickly—*throw*!

HODER: Did'st mark the place my throw was spent?
   I hear no sound of merriment . . .
   It was their wont with every blow—

   (Loki slips away)

   Silence . . . and a sound of woe . . .
   Loki!!! wherefore is this cry?

VOICE *(off)*: Dead!—Alas, why should he die?

   (Enter Odin and Hermod)

ODIN: Baldur is dead. A fateful dart
   On witless wing hath pierced his heart.
   Voiceless he sank upon his place,
   And smiling still his radiant face.

HODER: 'Twas *I*—'twas *I* who dealt the blow!

FRIGGA *(seeing dart)*: Alas,—the treacherous mistletoe!

HODER: What can I do? I'd gladly give
   My life for his, if he might live.

FRIGGA: Nought can'st thou do, blind as thou art,
   But he that hath vision and boldness of heart.
   Who of the gods will straightway ride
   To the darksome realm where the dead abide
   To offer a ransom at Hela's throne
   And bring me the soul of Baldur home?

HERMOD: Glad will I ride that fearful road
   To the realm of Hela's dread abode,
   But show me the way that I must take—
   I will risk all for Baldur's sake.

FRIGGA: Take Sleipnir, Odin's horse, and go
   Nine nights through valleys dark and low
   To the stream of death, that river cold
   And the bridge that is thatched with glittering gold.
   There sits a maid who guards the way,
   To her thy name and errand say,
   Then onward press to the gate of Hel,

There, tighten the girths of thy saddle well,
And, as swift from the bow as an arrow straight,
Put spurs to thy horse, and leap the gate.

(*Exit Hermod. Sound of horse galloping off. Enter gods, bearing body of Baldur*)

CHORUS: Down to the restless sea
Bear we the sacred earth.
Dark are the days to be,
Many the years of dearth.
High on the holy pyre
Deck we the dead with gold.
Rich is the flaming fire,—
Treasures of earth untold.
Into the deepening night
Launch we the flame afar.
Red are the waves alight,
Pale is the watching star.
Out on its bosom dark
Watch we the gentle deep
Rocking the last red spark
Softly to sleep.

(*Exeunt all, following chorus*)

CURTAIN

SCENE III

(IN FRONT OF CURTAIN)

(*Sounds of galloping, off, then a halt. Enter Hermod. A maiden appears, blocking his path*)

MAIDEN: Halt, traveller! Thy name and race!

HERMOD: Hermod the Bold. I go apace
To Hela's hall.

MAIDEN: Thy sounding tread
    Out-rings a multitude of dead.
    Thy cheeks bear not the hue of death ...
    What seek'st thou?

HERMOD: One that travelleth
    The same dark road of mortal woe.
    Of Baldur I would seek to know.

MAIDEN: I saw him pass,—nine days agone ...
    Ride on, bold traveller, ride on!

(Exit)

CURTAIN RISES

(Hela, on throne, surrounded by souls of the dead. Their faces are veiled)

CHORUS: We are the nameless dead
    Dim is our life, and grey.
    Sorrow and joy are fled,
    Night we know not, nor day,
    Dark we know not, nor light,
    Peace we know not, nor strife,
    Death we know not, nor life,—
    We are the dead.

(Sound of galloping, off, then loud knocking)

HELA: Who knocks unbid at Hela's Hall?

HERMOD *(off)*: I, Hermod, who doth humbly call
    Upon the Mother of the dead.

HELA: Enter, and say what must be said.

(Enter Hermod. Baldur raises arm in silent greeting)

HERMOD *(kneeling)*: Dread goddess of the world below,
    I come, a messenger of woe,
    From earth grown dark, a heaven grey,
    And grief that bears our life away.
    Thou hast bereft us of our light,
    Our well of truth, our vision bright ...

Our chiefest joy thou hast in thrall,
Baldur, most beautiful of all.

HELA: These things we know ... Make known thy quest.

HERMOD: That gods be glad, that earth be blessed,
I pray thee, yield the joy we lack
And give the soul of Baldur back!
No creature born of seas unknown,
No flower hid in forest deep,
No tree, nor flinty-hearted stone,
But one and all for Baldur weep.
The kings of earth, the gods on high,
The earth, the sea, the air, the sky,
All weep for Baldur. Grant us then
His ransomed spirit back again.

HELA: Do *all* things weep? Withholds no thing
Its dewy meed of sorrowing?
Is Baldur loved, as ye avow?
Then let the gods make trial now
Of every creature, quick or dead,
That ye may prove the words ye said.
If all things weep, Baldur shall go
Ransomed from the realms below.
But, lives one thing in earth or sky
That will his meed of tears deny—
Entreat no more at Hela's throne,
For Baldur shall remain our own.

HERMOD: Farewell! High hope shall spur me on,
And Baldur shall be free anon.

(*Exit Hermod. Baldur steps forward with raised hand, and remains during chorus*)

CHORUS: We are the nameless dead.
Dim is our life, and grey.
Sorrow and joy are fled,
Night we know not, nor day,
Dark we know not, nor light,

Peace we know not, nor strife,
Death we know not, nor life—
We are the dead.

SLOW CURTAIN

SCENE IV

The earth

(*Enter Thor, looking about him, then Hermod from opposite side*)

THOR: 'Tis here our meeting-place should be.
Hail, Hermod! Goes it well with thee?

HERMOD: I have spoken to the stones,
To pitiless cliffs—the fixéd bones
Of earth's fair flesh. All these did weep
The hidden tears that softly sleep
In rocks and stones neath winter's wing,
Till wakened by the touch of spring.

THOR: I strode the forests, tracked the bear,
The flaming tiger; broached the lair
Of sleepless lions. Wolves I saw—
Shadowy, on silent paw—
Leopards, spotted as the shade,
And snakes in secret shelter laid.
All creatures of the deathless wild
Wept unasked for Odin's child.

(*Enter Frigga, Odin, and other gods*)

FREYA: Fish, and monsters of the deep,
And wingéd birds for Baldur weep.

FRIGGA: The clouds have shed their showers for rue,
And plants have wept their latest dew.

ODIN: All men are weeping Baldur's death,
And Asgard dumbly sorroweth.

CHORUS: No creature born of seas unknown,
   No flower hid in forest deep,
   No tree, nor flinty-hearted stone,
   But one and all for Baldur weep.
   The kings of earth, the gods on high,
   The earth, the sea, the air, the sky,
   All weep for Baldur. To us then
   Baldur shall return again.

   (*Sound of shrill laughter*)

THOKK (*off*): What seek the gods in my domain?
   Doth it grow wearisome to reign
   In sunny Asgard?

THOR (*raising hammer*):   Only tears
   For Baldur, seek we. Keep thy jeers!

HERMOD: Why sittest thou athwart the sun,
   With darkened face, O aged one?
   Come, mingle thou thy woe with all
   Who weep him out of Hela's Hall.

   (*Enter Thokk*)

THOKK: Is Baldur dead? And do ye come
   For floods of tears to bear him home?
   I love him not, alive or dead.
   What matter, if his soul be fled?
   I weep him not, weep all who may.
   Let Hela keep her precious prey!

   (*Exit, laughing*)

THOR (*raising hammer*): 'Tis Loki,—'tis the wicked one!

ODIN (*restraining him*): Alas, alas, the deed is done . . .
   Baldur the Beautiful—my son!
              (Bows his head in sorrow).

CHORUS: Now comes, with heaven's darkened face
   The twilight of the gods apace.
   The serpent of the deep shall rise,

> The stars fall flaming from the skies,
> The sun grow dark and pallid night
> Glow with a red and awful light.
> Then blows the trumpet-blast afar
> That summons to the final war,
> The heavens are cloven, Hel set free,
> And earth sinks flaming in the sea.

(*The gods bow their heads*)

BALDUR'S *voice from afar off*:
> I see a Hall more golden-fair
> Than all the splendours of the sun,
> And earth, re-born in beauty, wear
> The dew of morning new-begun,
> And gods in glory reigning there,
> And hearts at peace, and warfare done—
> Then, when the earth with *love* shall burn
> I shall return— . . . I shall return.

(*The voice fades away*)

Chorus of gods (*raising their heads with a new joy*)
> Baldur the Beautiful, god of light,
> Robed in sunshine, peerless, bright,
> Pure of brow as the lily white,
> Gladden our hearts with thy golden light.

THOR AND THE GIANTS

(age 9–10)

In contrast to the previous play, this is a story of rollicking fun. Thor's magic hammer, by means of which he is able to defy the giants, the enemies of the gods, is stolen by one of them. The god Loki, the ever mischievous, is delighted for it gives him an opportunity to show his cunning, and he offers to fly to the dark and frosty giantland to retrieve the hammer. He finds the giant who had stolen it, but the price demanded by the giant for the restitution of the hammer is that he should have the goddess Freya as his bride. Loki returns with the message but Freya is furiously indignant and refuses to be the bride of such a creature. Then it is suggested that Thor himself should go, dressed as the bride. Thor is prevailed upon to agree and, much to his disgust, is clad in the bridal garments; then, accompanied by the delighted Loki dressed as "her" waiting-maid, they set off in Thor's flying chariot.

The giants are powerful but stupid, and the fun grows as the excited bridegroom is told of the approach of the chariot. Thor's gaucheries and quite unmaidenly behaviour under his bridal veil, while Loki scolds him in whispered asides and hops around making excuses to the wondering giant, bring the fun to its height—until, bursting with joy and pride, the giant orders the famous hammer to be brought and laid on the bride's lap, as his wedding gift to her. Then Thor, free at last to give vent to his feelings, puts his hammer to good use and slays the giants.

It is very important to choose a really lively, mischievous "Loki". There is usually one in a class.

SCENE I

Asgard

CHORUS OF GODS, ETC.:
>The sun has sunk in glory of gold,
>The wheeling ravens homeward fly.
>The shepherd brings his sheep to fold,
>And night breathes peace on earth and sky.
>Yet watch the gods from heights afar
>The fields of earth, and dale and hill.

The moon rides forth in her silver car.
The ordered heavens are sleepless still.
Peace on the earth, and power on high,
Who should the rule of the gods defy?

(*Exeunt. Enter Thrym, steals across stage, and returns with Thor's hammer. Exit*)

(*Thunder and lightning. Enter Loki*)

LOKI: Ah! Thor is angry. What's amiss
On such a peaceful night as this?

(*More violent thunder and lightning*)

Now, woe betide us! Here's a rage
That none in Asgard can assuage.
If only I could ferret out
What all the trouble is about
I'd have such fun his wrath to see. . . .

(*Thunder and lightning: Enter Thor*)

THOR: Loki! Thou son of treachery,
'Tis thou hast stolen it away!
Where hast thou laid it, serpent, say!

LOKI: Naught have I stolen, mighty Thor.
No deed have I to fear thee for!

THOR: Then, hearken to a thing unknown
In heaven or earth—my hammer's gone!

LOKI: Thy hammer! Gone! Without thy mace
Who shall withstand the giant race?

THOR: Well do I know it! . . . Who should dare
To steal it? Who is he?—and where?

LOKI: Peace! Let me think! . . . It seems to me
None but a giant could it be
Who seeks to rob thee of thy power.
Give me but wings, and I shall scour
Mid frost and darkness, mist and rime,

The length and breadth of Jotunheim.
There shall I trace thy hammer's flight.

(Enter Chorus)

CHORUS: What trouble stirs the gentle night?

LOKI: Trouble in plenty, woe on woe!
Thor's lost his hammer, and I go
To seek it in the realms below!
Good Freya, lend thy falcon wings,
And I shall do such *cunning* things!

FREYA: Is this a jest, or speaks he truth?

THOR: Alas, 'tis even so, in sooth.

FREYA: Then shall he have my falcon's dress.

ODIN: And we shall abide in readiness
Until thou tidings hast to tell.
Our fate is in thy hands.

ALL: Farewell!

(Dim out (to indicate passage of time))

CHORUS: The Fates with wise far-seeing ken
Spin the lives of gods and men.
Warp and woof, they weave the thread
For joy and woe, for hope and dread.
Comes the hour, the last of all,
The thread is cut—the leaf must fall.

FREYA: Here cometh Loki on the wing!

(Enter Loki)

LOKI: Peace, all is well: good news I bring.
Hither and thither, without a stop
I flew till I reached a mountain-top,
And there with his legs astride the crest
Sat Thrym the giant. I told my quest
And asked if he knew of a hammer lost
Anywhere in the realms of frost.

"In sooth" said Thrym, "a hammer I keep,
"Taken from Thor as he lay asleep."
"How clever!" said I, "What a jest to crack!
"And now let Thor have his plaything back."
"But nay," said Thrym, "the hammer I found
"Lies buried eight miles underground.
"There shall it lie until thou bring
"A worthy gift for such a thing.
"There in the earth shall the weapon bide
"Till thou bringest me Freya as my bride."

ALL: Freya!

LOKI: So let me lead thee by the hand.
A husband awaits thee in giantland!

FREYA: I—wed to a giant! Is *this* thy skill—
Thy boasted cunning? Without my will
Banished for ever from Asgard bright
To dwell with ugliness, cold and night!
Ne'er shall I take so foul a mate!

CHORUS: Alas, what then shall be our fate?
Soon shall the giants beat at our door
And gods in Asgard reign no more.

FRIGGA: Heimdal, thou guardian of our hold,
Hast thou no counsel to unfold?

HEIMDAL: Here is my rede. Let *strength* prevail.
Let *Thor* put on the bridal veil,
A woman's mantle to his knees,
And at his waist a bunch of keys,
A hood be folded round his head,—
And so go forth in Freya's stead.
Courage and strength he does not lack—
So may he win his hammer back.

THOR: *Dressed as a bride!*—for all to see!
A pretty maiden I should be!
I'll dare the giants to their very throats,
But ne'er will I hide in petticoats!

LOKI: Nay, Thor, but Heimdal's rede is wise.
I pray thee, think of this disguise
As but a way of entering in.
Then shalt thou soon thy hammer win.
And I shall come to give thee aid,
And be thy gentle waiting-maid.

CHORUS (*as they dress Thor and Loki*):
Dress the gentle bride,
Deck the maiden pale,
Modest blushes hide
'Neath the sheltering veil.
Hang the golden keys
From the girdle trim,
Shoulders to the knees
Drape the tender limb
Like a flower fair
On a slender stem,—
Crown the golden hair
With silver diadem.

MESSENGER: The chariot awaits the bride!

LOKI: Come, then, fair Freya,—let us ride!

(*Thor gives a roar of rage. Exit Thor and Loki*)

CURTAIN

SCENE II

Thrym's Castle

CHORUS OF GIANTS: Dark and gloomy is our home,
Awesome sounds our thund'rous tread.
Quakes the earth where'er we roam,
Fly our foes in fear and dread.
Gods we hate, and men are clods.
We shall conquer men and gods.

>   Now is mighty Thor undone.
>   Fast we shall his hammer hold.
>   So is half our battle won.
>   We are mighty, we are bold.
>   Let who will our strength defy,
>   We shall conquer earth and sky.

THRYM: Cattle and gold have I in store,
   Yet rich I'll be as ne'er before
   If Freya comes to be my bride,
   For she is worth all else beside.

(Enter servant)

SERVANT: O Thrym, against the evening sky
   Something hastening I espy.

THRYM: Is it an eagle on the wing?

SERVANT: Nay, 'tis a faster-moving thing.

THRYM: Comes it hither or goes it thence?

SERVANT: Indeed but it comes quickly hence,
   Borne on wings I cannot see. . . .
   A chariot it seems to be.

THRYM: A chariot? And can'st thou tell
   Who may ride in it, as well?

SERVANT: I see two figures, gleaming white—
   Two maidens—if I see aright,
   And one is tall, of seeming grace,
   A bridal veil before her face.

THRYM: 'Tis she! 'Tis she! my bride hath come!
   My giants, make her welcome home!
   Quick, spread the board with dainties fine—
   Fat roasted oxen, salmon, wine. . . .

SERVANT: The chariot is at the gate.

THRYM: Quick,—greet her with befitting state,
   And bring her gently here to me!

SERVANT: A handmaid must the other be,
And Freya—tall and strong of limb,—
A fitting bride for thee, O Thrym!
And now they reach the castle door,
They enter—and I see no more,
But hark! their feet upon the stair. . . .

THRYM: She comes! She comes! my giants, prepare,—
For Freya enters. . . .

(*Enter Thor and Loki*)

Come, fair bride
And sit, I pray thee, by my side.
Now let a *dainty* dish be laid,
Fitting for a tender maid.

(*Thor devours it in a few seconds and looks around for more*)

THOR (*to Loki*): This is no dish for hungry folk!

LOKI: Hush! murmur not beneath thy cloak!

(*Thor takes Thrym's fish, when he is not looking, and eats it*)

THRYM (*to Loki*): In troth, she is a maid of might!
Is this her usual appetite?

LOKI: Nay, but the thought of marrying thee
Hath so excited her that she
Hath eaten nought for seven days.
These are not her usual ways.

(*Thor, at last satisfied, leans back*)

THRYM: And now, fair Freya, by thy grace,
Let me see thy lovely face.

(*He lifts the edge of the veil. Thor gives him such a look that he draws back*)

(*to Loki*): Why do Freya's eyes so burn
That like a flame on me they turn?

LOKI: Her love for thee which burns always
Hath raged like fire these seven days!

THRYM: Then, let our wedding-troth be plighted,
    That hand in hand we be united.
    Bring forth my gift for all to see,
    And lay it on the maiden's knee.
    'Tis Thor's own plaything—now 'tis thine,—
    My wedding-gift, bethrothal sign.

THOR: And take *this* wedding-gift as *mine*! ! !

    (*Thor smites Thrym on the head, and then all the giants, who fall dead*)

LOKI: Ha, ha! fair Freya,—neatly done!

THOR: No more of that! The hammer's won.
    This woman's work—it had to be,—
    But speak no more of it to me!

                        (*Exeunt*)

CURTAIN

CHRISTMAS PLAY

THE WISE MEN'S WELL

(age 9–10)

This play is taken from a legend told by Selma Lagerlöf, the Swedish writer, in her book "Christ Legends". It tells of three wise men—at first not so very wise —who set off to find the baby Jesus. They have seen the star in the east, which, they believe, heralds the birth of a king who one day will rule the earth, and each hopes to be rewarded in some way for bringing this news to the father of the child, for they picture an earthly king, born in a palace. They come to the stable but think this cannot be the birthplace of a royal person, and so turn away. They lose their way, the star deserts them, and in despair and suffering they begin to realise their folly and greed. At last they come to a well in the desert where they sink down to rest and refresh their thirst. As one looks down into the water he sees reflected in it the star they had lost and looking up they see it shining again in the sky. Repentant, they turn again to follow it once more to the stable.

The play begins, however, many years later. The well is still there, but a terrible drought threatens to dry it up. Meanwhile, the Drought in person— the spirit of all dry-heartedness—gloats over the dying well and jeers at those who come to draw from it. At length three strangers arrive and ask why it is called the "Wise Men's Well" and the Drought obligingly tells the story which is meanwhile enacted by the three wise men. The three strangers, however, prove to be the original wise men now come down from Paradise in gratitude to save the well from perishing. They pour into it water from heaven, and the Drought flees in despair.

CHORUS: This is a legend of days gone by,
    When the sun shone fierce in a flaming sky,
    And the earth's fair face was a wrinkled crust,
    And the flowers lay dead, and the streams were dust,
    And the cattle, lowing on hill and plain,
    Bent their heads to the soil in vain,
    And all things cried with a voice of death,
    While the Drought arose with his fiery breath
    To blast the wells of the wasted land,

And bathe his feet in the burning sand.

At last to the Wise Men's Well he came,
Along the road to Bethlehem.

DROUGHT: All things are dust, and to dust return . . .
 So shall I wither, bleach and burn
 Till all the land is dry and dead,
 Then peace shall reign, when life is fled.
 I hate the sound of streams that run,
 Dancing defiance to the sun.
 I hate the sap that flows in spring
 To bring the buds to blossoming.
 I hate the rain that feeds the sod
 And heals the place where I have trod . . .
 Here is a well—what hope hast thou
 To save thy waters from me now?
 Dost look for some mysterious flow
 To feed thy being there below?

WELL: Dread spirit, thou may'st rest content.
 Alas, my life is all but spent.
 No deed can save me, nor device,
 But some well-spring from Paradise.

DROUGHT: And that shall surely not befall
 Since now I hold the clouds in thrall.
 Dear Well, I pity thee—and hate
 To leave thee to thy lonely fate,
 But on thy brink I'll gladly stop,
 And watch thee dying, drop by drop.

(*Enter young woman with pitcher. She sets it down and lets down the bucket into the well*)

DROUGHT (*continues*): What profit, damsel, wilt thou get
 From all thy toil,—save dust and sweat?

GIRL: I come to draw fresh water, first,—
 My father, Sir, is sore athirst,—
 Then must I water well the cow,
 No dewy grass is left her now.

DROUGHT: Thou wastest both thy strength and time.

(Girl draws up bucket)

GIRL: Alas, 'tis nought but mud and slime!

DROUGHT: Aye—so it is!—a pity, now,
    For both thy father and the cow!

(Exit young woman)

(Enter old woman with pitcher)

OLD WOMAN *(sits down exhausted on well's edge)*:
    Ah! I have reached thee, well, at length!
    Good Sir, if yet thou hast the strength,
    Would'st draw the heavy bucket up?
    A cup of water! Just one cup!

DROUGHT *(grinning)*: Gladly (for every drop we spend
    Will bring it nearer to an end.)

(Draws up bucket)

OLD WOMAN: Give me to drink. I die of thirst.

DROUGHT: 'Twere best to look inside it first.

(Old woman glances into bucket)

OLD WOMAN: 'Tis only mud. The well is dry!
    God send us rain, or else we die!

(EXIT)

(Enter old man)

OLD MAN: God save thee, stranger. Can'st thou tell
    If there be water in this well?

DROUGHT: None! for the last black drop is gone
    To mock the death of an aged crone.
    No rain shall fall, and no stream shall run,
    Nothing shall live 'neath the burning sun.
    Nothing shall be, save dust and bones,
    And the seas of sand, and the silent stones.

OLD MAN: What man art thou that dost rejoice
  With gleaming eye and ringing voice?

DROUGHT: I am the Drought—long feared of old,
  My breath is hot, yet my heart is cold.
  Return, old man, to thy home and die,
  For the well of life is parched and dry.

(Exit Old man)

CHORUS: Night falls, but brings no cooling breath,
  Hot shadows climb the weary hill,
  The jackal howls his hymn of death,
  The streams are dumb. The woods are still.
  But see—on yonder starry crest
  All silvered by the moon, we scan—
  With kingly riders richly dressed—
  A bright and lordly caravan.
  A heaven-descended host it seems,
  Born from the light of the silver beams.

DROUGHT: Here comes a cavalcade of thirst!
  Drink then of dryness till ye burst!

(Enter three strangers, followed by servants)

1ST STRANGER: Sir, in a distant land we dwell
  And come to seek the Wise Men's Well.
  Is this in truth the Well we seek?

DROUGHT: Aye, 'tis the well of which ye speak.
  At least, men call it so today.
  Tonight 'twill surely dry away.

2ND STRANGER: But is this not a sacred well
  Which ne'er runs dry?—or can'st thou tell
  Whence it should earn so great a name?

DROUGHT: Sacred or not—'tis all the same.
  For those three men who were so wise
  Are long ago in Paradise.

(The strangers exchange glances)

THE WISE MEN'S WELL

3RD STRANGER: Dost know the tale of this ancient well?

DROUGHT: Of every spring the tale I can tell—
 Of every river beneath the sun,—
 As well as of rivers that *used* to run.

3RD STRANGER: Then let us rest and hear the story
 Of the Wise Men's Well and its ancient glory.

(While the Drought tells the story, the three Wise Men are seen asleep in the background)

DROUGHT: In a desert city there lived three men,
 Wise they were and far famed, but then
 One was old, one had leprosy,
 And the third was blacker than ebony.
 So few came questioning at their door,
 And the three wise men became so poor,
 That now no sheltering house they kept,
 But cold on a roof each night they slept.
 One night—'twas long and long ago—
 When the stars like lamps hung all aglow—
 And the waves of light surged far and free,
 And the skies were deep as a boundless sea—
 One of the sleepers awoke, and cried
 To the humble brethren by his side:—

1ST WISE MAN (*Leper*):
 Brothers, awake, awake, I say!
 The heavens are gleaming as if 'twere day.
 And lo, in the east, a rosy light—
 What should that mean—do I see aright?

2ND WISE MAN (*Negro*):
 Nay,—'tis a star—I see it arise
 Brightest of all in the radiant skies.
 What should it be—my brothers—this thing?

3RD WISE MAN (*Oldest*):
 'Tis the star of the mighty, the star of a King!
 A King who shall compass the earth in his sway,
 A King of all kings has been born this day!

1ST WISE MAN: To whom shall we tell it—to whom make it known?

2ND WISE MAN: To the king—the child's father—and to him alone.

3RD WISE MAN: Come, let us set forth, and make no more delay,
Let us follow the star till the breaking of day.

(*They set out, and speak as they walk*)

1ST WISE MAN: Should we not be glad, that God has so planned
To reveal this to us, alone, in the land?

2ND WISE MAN: He has counted us worthy—so poor as we are,
To carry the news of this wonderful star.

3RD WISE MAN: Perchance it may be that his father, the king,
Shall give us rewards for the message we bring.

1ST WISE MAN: Aye,—so it may happen! and we shall no more
Beg for our bread at the gate or the door.

2ND WISE MAN: How grand will the palace appear in our eyes,
And the cradle of gold in which the Babe lies!

3RD WISE MAN: The richest reward shall he give us, all three,
Twenty purses of silver at least, it should be.

DROUGHT: The star led them safely—nor hunger nor thirst
Afflicted their journey—though I did my worst!
But their hearts 'neath the touch of my delicate hand,
Grew dry as the desert and barren as sand.

1ST WISE MAN: Nay, gold and *not* silver—we surely shall get,
And chains for our necks with rich jewels beset!

2ND WISE MAN: If the king will reward us as well as he can,
He will saddle with gold a right long caravan!

3RD WISE MAN: Behold,—the star rests. But no palace I see!
Where in this town should a king's dwelling be?

1ST WISE MAN: Look well where it stops, then if we be able
To ask them our way—why it's only a stable!

2ND WISE MAN: Most surely, my brothers, have we been beguiled.
Here is nought but a shepherd, his wife and their child!

3RD WISE MAN: Has God brought us hither that we should but mock,
With praises and honours, a son of the flock?

1ST WISE MAN: Howe'er could this child become King of the earth
With his dwelling a stable, and lowly his birth?

2ND WISE MAN: Let us waste no more speech on so paltry a thing,
But seek for a dwelling more fit for a king.

(They continue their journey)

CHORUS: But yet they had not wandered far,
When looking upward to the star
Where once in glory it had shone—
They found their guiding light had gone.
And now in suffering deep they roam,
With hearts despairing far from home.
For now they clearly understand
That they have broken God's command.
At length, bewildered, stricken, dumb,
Toward this very well they come.

3RD WISE MAN: Here is sweet water that may give
Our souls new birth, that we may live.

1ST WISE MAN: 'Twere best to soothe our sorrows thus,
For God has quite forgotten us.

2ND WISE MAN: This well is like a mirror bright.
See what shines here with rosy light!

3RD WISE MAN: It is the star which shines again.
Thanks be to God for all our pain!

1ST WISE MAN: Come, brothers, let us go once more
And humbly knock at the stable door.

2ND WISE MAN: Perchance the Child is yet within
And God has wiped away our sin.

3RD WISE MAN: And though the way be long and hard,
We ask no other for reward.

(They return to the stable)

CHORUS: And now they kneel before the King
    And humbly give their offering
    Of gold and myrrh and frankincense
    Seeking no kind of recompense.
    But Mary speaks to them anew:—

MARY: My Son will now give gifts to you.
    To him who is old and feeble of ways,
    Youth shall be given, and length of days.
    To him who is black and strange of face,
    A fair white form of beauty and grace.
    And he who has suffered the leper's dole
    He shall henceforth be clean and whole.

DROUGHT: And that, good Sirs, is the tale I tell
    Of what was *once* the Wise Men's Well.

1ST STRANGER: And well hast thou told it. But have they forgot,—
    Those three wise men,—the blessing it brought?

2ND STRANGER: And should not this well remain to show
    That in humble hearts the star will glow?

3RD STRANGER: And dost thou think that thankfulness dies
    With those who dwell in Paradise?

(*They group themselves around the well, and as they speak, they pour into it heavenly waters*)

ALL THREE: This well shall live, and here we bring
    Sweet water from the heavenly spring!

DROUGHT (*in fear and terrible anguish*):
    Ye are the Three Wise Men! I plead—
    Let me not see this dreadful deed!

                (*flees shrieking*)

GILGAMESH AND EABANI

(age 10–11)

This little play represents, in a very brief form, some of the salient incidents from the Epic of Gilgamesh, one of the most important literary products of Babylonia, discovered among the royal collection of tablets in the library of Assur-bani-pal, king of Assyria in the seventh century B.C. It tells of a conqueror and tyrant, Gilgamesh, believed to be more than human and said to be two-thirds a god, who, having captured the city of Erech, forces all the able-bodied men to build the great city wall. The people sigh under their burdens and call upon the goddess Aruru to create a being who might become a rival to Gilgamesh and conquer him. The goddess hears their prayer and creates a strange creature, Eabani (also called Enkidu) who, quite primitive and wild, lives with the beasts of field and forest. He is guided by a beautiful maiden to meet Gilgamesh with whom he fights. Gilgamesh overcomes Eabani, but they become fast friends and depart together to seek adventures. On their return from slaying a monster in the cedar forests they are met by the goddess Ishtar who tries to woo Gilgamesh; but Gilgamesh, knowing the tragic fate of her former lovers, and reminding her of these, spurns her offer. Enraged, Ishtar lays a curse upon the city, which results in the death of Eabani. Gilgamesh, in despair at losing his friend and brought thus face to face with death, determines to set out in search of eternal life. He journeys westwards, and after many severe trials, reaches the dwelling of his ancestor, Ut-Napishtim (the Babylonian Noah) who is now a god. Of him he seeks the secret of immortality. Ut-Napishtim sets him a test, in which he fails; and at this point the play ends. Later, on returning home, he is permitted to view the shade of Eabani who tells him of the sad fate endured by the dead. This ends the Epic.

This story typifies a period when men began to fear death as leading to a dim and dreary after-life, later held also by the Greeks as the "realm of the shades". The play, however, ends with a note of hope for the future.

SCENE I

BUILDING THE CITY WALL

CHORUS: Work, my brothers, work,
    Build the bastion-wall.

Soon the winging dark
Spreads her blinding pall.
Pile the trusty brick
Baked beneath the sun,
Dug from clinging earth
Where the rivers run.
Raise our earthen shield
High against the foe.
Build a house of peace
In a world of woe.
Soon the winging dark
Spreads her blinding pall.
Work, my brothers, work,
Build the bastion-wall.

1ST BUILDER: O, weary is my heart and sore.
    Let darkness come,—I'll work no more!

2ND BUILDER: 'Tis many moons since last I knew
    A bed unwetted by the dew,
    But night breathes peace upon our scars,
    And rich our canopy of stars.

3RD BUILDER: I would I saw my house once more,
    The glowing hearth, protecting door,
    My children scrambling on the floor.
    They wait in vain my coming home.

4TH BUILDER: My plough's unyoked, my cattle roam
    Through fruitless fields.

5TH BUILDER: My new-wed spouse
    Seeks shelter in her father's house.

1ST BUILDER: Let folly cease! Why should we make
    A city for a tyrant's sake?
    Raise ramparts to exalt his pride,
    That men may know he lived,—and died?

3RD BUILDER: Died? Shall such a path be trod
    By Gilgamesh—two-thirds a god?

2ND BUILDER: He is the shepherd of his folk,
　　　　　　And guards our peace. We bear his yoke—
　　　　　　But share his glory.

4TH BUILDER:　　　　　　　　　　　Let it be!
　　　　　　I'd sell *my* glory to be free!

5TH BUILDER: Come, pray the Mother of mankind
　　　　　　To succour us—a champion find,
　　　　　　With arm as strong, as brave a breast,
　　　　　　To strive with him—and bring us rest.

CHORUS: Mother goddess, who didst make
　　　　Living clay in mortal mould,
　　　　Shape for us, thy children's sake,
　　　　Man courageously ensouled.
　　　　Raise anew a soul of worth
　　　　Wrapped in wisdom-shapen earth,—
　　　　Thou who wrought in days of old,
　　　　Living clay in mortal mould.

　　　　　　　　　(Enter Gilgamesh)

GILGAMESH: How now, why stand ye idle there?
　　　　　Think ye to build a wall by prayer?
　　　　　The gods give strength to *willing* hands,
　　　　　Nor succour him who idle stands
　　　　　With empty palms towards the sky—

CHORUS: Let the king hearken to our cry!
　　　　We are as dust beneath his feet,
　　　　Yet have we wives and children sweet
　　　　Who look to us as we to gods—

GILGAMESH: What are ye all but earthen clods
　　　　　To serve *my* will? And what your wives?
　　　　　In these my hands lie your trembling lives!
　　　　　To share my glory were ye made,
　　　　　Your hands to build, to grasp the spade.
　　　　　Work ye, nor murmur at your lot,
　　　　　Lest, like the dogs, ye die, forgot.—

I speak, the lord of your souls and flesh,
I, the conqueror, Gilgamesh!

(Builders resume work)

CHORUS: Work, my brothers, work ... etc.

CURTAIN

SCENE II

The Coming of Eabani

CHORUS: Aruru, the goddess, heard
Shaped a being strange and new,
Dwelt he with the forest herd,
'Mid the roving flocks he grew.
Long his hair as woman-kind,
Dark his skin with hair be-clad.
Ate and drank he with the kine,
With the fishes was he glad.
Came to him a maiden fair,
Sought him in the forest deep,
Where the cattle, unaware,
Kneel to drink at hour of sleep.
Gazed he on her beauty bright,
All amazed at form so fresh,
Followed her, a guiding light,
To meet with Gilgamesh.

(Enter Maiden, followed by Eabani. He gazes round, crowd shrinks from him in awe)

(Enter Gilgamesh. Eabani springs to block his path)

GILGAMESH: And who art thou who thinks to stand
Athwart my path? And what strange land
Hath given thee shape? Art thou a man?

EABANI: Aye, more than one. My life began
          Among the woods. I am the child
          Of Wisdom and the stormy wild.
          I eat of herbs, I drink of streams,
          And weave my wonder-working dreams.

GILGAMESH: Here are no dreams of dim delight.
          What seek'st thou?

EABANI: I would know thy might,
          And prove my strength in mortal fight!

                    (*They close and wrestle*)

CHORUS: Now they struggle, strain and sway.
          Eabani hath his way!
          Now hath Gilgamesh the grip,
          Knee to knee, and hip to hip,
          Muscles tighten, sinews crack,
          Thrusting shoulders, bending back.
          Tug and tussle, turn and twist,
          Arm and thigh and foot and wrist—
          Eabani weakens—see
          His bending knee, his bending knee!
          Slowly sinks he to the earth,
          Crushed by one of greater worth.

GILGAMESH: Grieve not, nor sink in hopeless shame,
          For thine shall be a glorious name.
          Ne'er have I fought so strong a foe.
          Arise, and welter not in woe.
          Come, be my friend, and thou and I
          Shall seek adventure. Eastward lie
          The forest lands, the cedars tall
          Where long a monster hath in thrall
          The woods around. Him shall we slay.
          Come, gather glory while we may!

                    (*Exeunt*)

CHORUS: They sought the monster, him they slew,
          'Mid the waving forests deep,
          Where the lordly cedars grew

And the hills their silence keep.
Came they to the city proud,
All arrayed as brother kings,
Everlasting friendship vowed,
Rulers twain of lordly things.
But Ishtar, goddess, fair of old,
Looking from her heavenly place,
Gazed on Gilgamesh the bold
And loved his manly grace.

(*Enter Gilgamesh and Eabani, and Ishtar meeting them*)

ISHTAR: Hail, Gilgamesh, thou god of men,
Hail, monster-slayer, glorious grown,
Long have I looked, and looked again
For one to share my throne.
Be thou my husband, dwell with me,
Where cedars yield their perfume sweet.
Of gold thy chariot shall be,
And kings shall kiss thy feet.

GILGAMESH: I trust thee not; is not thy love
A hawk that murmurs as a dove?
A tiger in a heifer's dress?
A ruin that is shelterless?
Thy former lovers—where are they?
The bird that moans with broken wing?
The lion trapped in pit of clay?
The shepherd's wolfish wandering?
At length, bewitched, or maimed, or dead,
So fare those whom thou dost wed!

ISHTAR: Cursed be this city for thy sake!
Cursed be the ramparts thou dost make!
Cursed be the lives that dwell therein!
Cursed be thy folk, and cursed thy kin!
An instant plague shall waste their flesh,
And thou shalt know bitterness, Gilgamesh!

(*Exit*)

(*Eabani sways and falls*)

GILGAMESH: Why liest thou, Eabani, there?
　　　　　What sleep hath seized upon thy soul?
　　　　　Dark is thy face, and unaware
　　　　　Thou gazest on some nameless goal.
　　　　　My voice thou hearest not, my hand
　　　　　Stirs not thy sense, nor moves thy will.
　　　　　Dost wander in some distant land—
　　　　　With heart so still?
　　　　　Eabani, thou art dead!
　　　　　Dead, my lion-hearted friend!
　　　　　No more our battle-paths to tread,
　　　　　No more thy huntsman's bow to bend.
　　　　　How shall I walk my life alone?
　　　　　How go unfriended all the way,
　　　　　Till I too lie, with face of stone,
　　　　　And coldly mingle with the clay?
　　　　　I will not die, and be as thou,
　　　　　With dark corruption in my breast,
　　　　　But haste—a lamp upon my brow—
　　　　　To seek the wisdom of the west.
　　　　　There shall I find, come woe, come strife,
　　　　　The secret of immortal life!

(Exit)

CURTAIN

SCENE III

GILGAMESH'S QUEST

Open space beside the home of Ut-Napishtim and his wife

UT-NAPISHTIM: Who may this urgent stranger be,
　　　　　　Hasting hither on the sea?

WIFE: His vessel I have watched afar
　　　Where the darkest billows are.

UT-NAPISHTIM: It is no man of common clay
    Who dares so perilous a way.

(*Enter Gilgamesh*)

Why so wasted thou, and pale,
Thy face cast down, thy strength undone?
What sorrow doth thy soul bewail,
Unhappy one?

GILGAMESH: I loved a friend, and he is dead,
    His heart hath dwindled into dust;
    I feared to look on death, and fled,
    Lest I too in the earth be thrust
    And share the common fate of men
    To rise no more again.
    Thou wert a man, and now a god,
    My very ancestor thou art.
    And have I not the pathway trod
    That leads to an immortal heart?
    The mountains have I dared, and know
    How fierce the wings of darkness beat.
    The sea of Death I sailed, and lo,
    I stand unconquered at thy feet.
    Here, Ut-Napishtim, am I come
    To seek the way of lasting life.
    Speak! unless the gods be dumb,
    And hearken not to human strife.

UT-NAPISHTIM: On earth there dwells no lasting thing.
    The gods, who gave their living breath
    To slave and warrior and king,
    Rule destiny and death.
    Thou can'st not flee thy mortal fate,
    Nor know thy death's appointed date.

GILGAMESH: Thou wert a man and did'st not die,
    Though mortal in thy flesh as I!

UP-NAPISHTIM: Then must thou show thy spirit's power,
    Six days and seven nights to keep

Thy soul from slumber, hour on hour,
For gods know nought of sleep.

GILGAMESH: I will abide both night and day!

WIFE: The winds of sleep are on their way.

(*Enter the four winds, who dance round Gilgamesh*)*

CHORUS: Softly stealing, the winds of sleep,
Wrap his soul in a slumber deep,
Sweetly soothe his sorrowing breast,
Swiftly shroud him in dreamless rest,
Still his voice and veil his eyes,
Waft him on wings to the silent skies.
Softly stealing, the winds of sleep,
Wrap his soul in a slumber deep.

(*Gilgamesh succumbs and falls to the ground in a deep sleep*)

WIFE: Poor wanderer with drooping brow,
No hope of victory is thine.
Dark is the path of such as thou
Who seek the way divine.

(*With Chorus, off*): The light upon the morning hills
Grows dim, and men shall miss their way,
Until a newer dawn, which fills
The earth with everlasting day.
Then shall the traveller have light,
And darkness pass away.

CURTAIN

* For "dance" read "perform Eurythmy" in Rudolf Steiner schools.

THE HALL OF JUDGMENT

(age 10–11)

The ancient Egyptians had a very clear picture of their beliefs concerning the life after death. In the Hall of Judgment the newly departed soul was judged by the gods, and if his life on earth was found worthy—his heart being weighed in the scales against the Feather of Truth—he was allowed to ascend into the Fields of Peace, there to dwell with the gods; but if he was proved unworthy, he was thrown to a monster who devoured him.

The play shows how an upright and innocent man, caught in a trap by his wicked brother and condemned to death for an apparent attempt on the life of Pharaoh, is misjudged on earth, while the gods judge him truly as he is. This last scene is taken from the Egyptian Book of the Dead, and if acted with the dignity and calmness appropriate to it, can form an impressive contrast to the tragic story which precedes it.

SCENE I

ANI'S HOUSE

(Ahuri, his wife, seated, sewing. Maati, his little girl, is on the floor, listening to a story)

MAATI: Mother! Go on with the story about the Underworld.

AHURI: Then, as the Sun, the boat of Ra,
    Sinks down beyond the western floor,
    The thronging souls of all the dead
    Stand trembling at the dreaded door.
    For here the secret waters flow
    Into the underworld below.
    At length the sacred ship they hail
    And now they hasten to embark
    On Ra's own boat wherein they sail
    Through twelve divisions of the dark,
    By fearsome cliffs where serpents lour

THE HALL OF JUDGMENT

    Seeking what souls they may devour,
    And in the waters dark, the while,
    Lies hid the loathsome crocodile.
    Until at midnight looms the wall
    Of Amentet, the Judgment Hall.

(Pause)

MAATI: Go on! Tell me—what happens then?

AHURI: Here must be judged the souls of men.
    Here sits Osiris on his throne,
    And here must stand each soul alone,
    To answer for his earthly days.
    And now the god, Anubis, weighs
    Each heart upon the balance, lays
    The feather of Truth upon the scale
    To weigh the heart, and if it fail
    To weigh as much, then shall that soul
    Be parted from his heavenly goal
    And straightway to a monster fed.
    But he, the true of heart, is led
    Through darkness into light that yields
          Peace, mid the Everlasting Fields.

MAATI: Are many eaten by the beast?

AHURI: How should I know, child? Some, may be.

MAATI: Should *I* make him a worthy feast?

AHURI *(smiling)*: No, hardly enough for such as he!
    But now, *three* monsters must be fed—
    Your father, you and I. Let's spread
    Our evening meal.

(They prepare to go out)

Enter Servant

SERVANT: My lady, stay—
    A stranger stands who bids me say
    That he would speak with you awhile.

AHURI: Go, bid him come.

(Enter Hotep)

HOTEP: Is this the house of Ani, Scribe,
  One time in Pharaoh's court?

AHURI: It is.
  He *is* at Pharaoh's court, and I
  Am Ahuri, his wife.

HOTEP: Good lady, I am named Hotep,
  And I am Ani's brother.

AHURI: I thought that Ani had but one
  Nor knew he had another.

HOTEP: No more does he. For I am dead
  These many years, it has been said.
  Good lady, let me but relate
  The curious story of my fate.
  Then you will quickly understand
  The matters that I have in hand.
  Long years ago—fifteen, may be—
  I and my brother kept the key
  Of Pharaoh's private treasury.
  We were the guardians of his gold,
  And none knew what he had in hold
  Save us—not even he, the King,
  But we had count of everything.
  Now one of us in turn, each day,
  Counted exactly all that lay
  Within that royal treasure store,
  Then shot the bolts and sealed the door.
  One day, my brother—'twas his turn—
  Found that a certain golden urn,
  Filled to the brim with jewels rare,
  Had vanished into empty air.
  Of robbers there was not a token.
  The door was locked, the seal unbroken.
  "'Tis some magician's work," said I.
  "Say naught to Pharaoh, let it lie,

The king will neither know nor care
What is here, or what is there."
But straight to Pharoah he must go.
" 'Tis right," said he, "the king should know."
The king was wroth and said, in brief,
That one of us must be the thief.
"If thief I be," my brother cries,
"May great Ra smite me from the skies!"
"If thief *I* be," likewise I said,
"May these stones fall upon my head!"
And even as I spoke that word
A loose stone, shaken by a bird,
Fell from the open colonnade
And I was mute and senseless laid.
"The gods have spoken!", cried they all,
And Pharoah's voice rang through the hall
"Let him be banished from the land".....
I have returned, and here I stand.

AHURI: But it is death to disobey
The word of Pharoah.

HOTEP: So it may.
But if my brother will repent
His sending me to banishment
Through foolish haste and needless fear...

                (*Enter Ani*)

See, brother, who awaits you here!

ANI: My brother Hotep! Is it so?
Whence come you?

HOTEP: From the realms below!
You thought me dead—but here you see
I'm as alive as I can be.
Are you not glad to see my face?
You give no brotherly embrace!

ANI: Know you not that the path you tread
Needs but one step till you be dead?

HOTEP: Not if my brother and his spouse
    Will give me shelter in their house.

ANI: And think you that of this no breath
    Will reach the ear of Pharaoh? Death
    My own reward shall likewise be.
    Then, what the gain to you—and me?

HOTEP: Hearken, my friend, and have no fear.
    Let someone speak in Pharaoh's ear
    That Hotep's heart doth in him burn
    Once more to Egypt to return,
    And, though he suffers banishment,
    That he indeed is innocent.
    See, I am rich—and you, a scribe,
    Know well the uses of a bribe.

ANI: So I must bribe a man to say
    'Twas *I* who stole the urn away!
    This is the root of your intent.

HOTEP: Nay, brother, 'twas not what I meant.
    It happened all so long ago—
    No man can say where gold may go.
    Remember, rather, 'twas your will
    And thoughtless haste that brought this ill.
    I do but ask for your support—
    You have much influence at court—
    To right the folly of the past
    And pay your debt to me—at last.

ANI: I owe no debt to any man.
    But now two deeds I have to scan—
    Either I plead for Pharaoh's grace
    Or thrust you from my dwellingplace.
    The first may bring me death, the other
    I may not do unto a brother ...
    Dear wife—shall danger be our choice?
    Or has your heart another voice?

AHURI: Come, let us sup.

(Exeunt all but Maati)

THE HALL OF JUDGMENT

MAATI (*acting the story told by her mother*):
  Anubis—hast thou weighed the heart of Hotep?
  Throw him to the monster!

CURTAIN

SCENE II

The Same

Three days later

(*The stage is empty. On a small table lies a golden casket. Enter Maati. She sees the casket and tiptoes towards it, looks at it, lifts the lid and peeps inside*)

MAATI: Oh! What a lovely box is here!
  All of gold and shining clear,
  Who can have brought it? What's inside?
  Jewels! and—

(*She gives a little scream and runs to a corner where she remains frightened and unnoticed*)

(*Enter Ani and Hotep*)

HOTEP: Here is the casket. It is meet
  We lay this gift at Pharaoh's feet,
  Or, better, place it in his hands
  Trusting that he understands
  We do but show our thankfulness
  That he has pitied my distress
  And pardoned me. But 'ere we go
  To stand before him, we should know
  Which of us shall offer it.
  Does it not seem to you unfit
  That I should give this to my Lord,
  As 'twere a bribe or a reward?
  Better that you the gift should bear
  Since you gain naught from the affair.

ANI: There is some truth in what you say.
Give me the box. Let us away.

(*Exeunt Ani and Hotep*)

MAATI (*cries*): Mother! Mother! (*runs out*)
Mother!! Mother! ! !

CURTAIN

SCENE III

PHARAOH'S COURT

(*Pharaoh on throne. On either side fanbearers. Chancellor. Scribes. Courtiers, Guards. Among these, on right, is a mother (a peasant woman) and her young son. On left is a man, also a peasant. Pharaoh is judging a dispute between them*)

WOMAN: And this, O Pharaoh, hath he done—
All that belongs unto my son—
Our land, our house, our cattle,—all
He seizes. Neither roof nor wall
Have we for shelter, corn nor bread.
O Pharaoh, thou the fountainhead,
The river of just deeds, do now
Restore our house and land.

PHARAOH: Art thou
A widow?

WOMAN: Yea, and this my son—
All that I have, my only one.

PHARAOH (*to man*): And did'st thou take the woman's land?

MAN: My lord, let Pharaoh understand,
I am her husband's brother, he—
The lad—too young for husbandry,
Too weak to plough and till and sow . . .

BOY: Thou liar! Since a year ago
  I've done it all!

MAN: I did but go
  To help my sister in her need.

BOY: This is no name for such a deed!
  He is a thief, a cheat, a liar!

  (*Chancellor, who all this time has been handling a scroll in an agitated way, breaks in*)

CHANCELLOR: Need we go further, Pharaoh, sire?
  Some matters here of great import
  Must be made known to all the court.

PHARAOH (*to man*): We shall inquire into your deeds—
  But let this woman have her needs
  Of food and shelter until then.
  Tomorrow you will come again.

  (*Exeunt man, woman and son. The boy shakes his fist at the man*)

CHANCELLOR: My lord, grave news has come to hand.
  An army marches on our land.
  The people of the south draw near,
  Our borders are attacked, and here
  Great Pharaoh's life, our spies report,
  Is threatened in his very court!

(*Courtiers and guards* (*grasping weapons*): What!
      (*looking around*)

PHARAOH: Our armies there are well bestowed.
  First let us finish with this load
  Of duties for today. Who waits
  Next in order at the gates?

CHANCELLOR: My lord, 'tis Ani and his brother.
  After these, there is no other.

PHARAOH: Bring them.

  (*An officer goes out and brings in Ani and Hotep. Hotep takes his place, right, and Ani, left. They bow*)

> Thou, Hotep, art here
> To ask for pardon, word most dear
> To all who stumble by the way,
> Yet, easy for a king to say.
> If I do say it, let it be
> A seal upon thy loyalty
> To Egypt and to Egypt's crown.
> Thou art pardoned. Set it down. (*To Chancellor*)

(*Hotep bows low, and slinks away, unnoticed*)

ANI: O, Sire, our gratitude to show,
    Grant us that we may bestow
    A humble gift. This box of gold,
    Like to that urn in days of old,
    With jewels filled, may wipe away
    All the sins of yesterday.
    I pray thee, Sire, let this express
    Our loyalty and thankfulness.

(*He hands the box to the Chancellor, who is about to hand it to Pharaoh, when Ahuri rushes into the court*)

AHURI: Touch it not, Pharaoh, death lies there
    Within that box! My lord, I swear
    This is no deed of ours. O spare
    My husband. Whence and how it came
    I know not, nor whose is the blame.
    By chance, the youngest of my girls. . . .

(*Chancellor opens box, shuts it quickly, and lays it on table*)

CHANCELLOR: A deadly snake among the pearls!
    This, Sire, is what your spies foretold—
    The threatening of thy life. Behold,
    These are the culprits. Hold them fast!
    And into prison have them cast.

(*Guards seize Ani*)

COURTIER (*on right*): Sir, the brother is not there—
    Hotep is gone, we know not where.

CHANCELLOR: Send guards to follow him! O Sire,
   What, for *this* man, is thy desire?

PHARAOH (*to Ani*) (*rising*):
   My servant and my one-time friend,
   Canst thou say aught that could defend
   Thy soul before this dreadful deed?

ANI: Pharaoh, I can do naught but plead
   My innocence. I humbly swear
   I knew of naught but jewels there.
   I am thy faithful servant still.
   Do thou according to thy will.

PHARAOH: Know thou this day our spies have shown
   A plot against our very throne—
   That Pharaoh's life in danger lay
   From those around him. Canst thou say
   "I know not of it, nor of those
   Who at this hour are Egypt's foes"?
   Thy brother comes with twisted mouth
   Straight from the Kingdom of the South
   To plead for pardon and so bring
   A way of death unto the king.
   He has had shelter from thy roof,
   Thou bringest death on his behoof.
   What further need be thought or said?
   Thyself shalt stand among the dead
   This night, when darkness spreads her pall,
   Within Osiris' Judgment Hall.

   (*Ani is led away by the guards, followed by Ahuri crying*)

AHURI: Ani, Ani, Ani!

CURTAIN

SCENE IV

Hall of Judgment

(Osiris on throne. Behind him Isis and Nephthys: Before him Horus, Anubis, Thoth: At back, the gods. A voice is heard off)

ANI (*off*): Homage to thee, O Ra,
　　Who risest in thy glory.
　　Thou rulest in the heavens,
　　And when the shadows come
　　Thou carest for the souls
　　Of them that wait in darkness
　　And bearest them in thy boat
　　Safe to the Hall of Judgment.
　　Homage to thee, O Ra.

GODS: Who is the wand'rer whose voice
　　Praiseth the sun?
　　Alone in Amentet we reign,
　　Judging the dead.
　　Powerless is Ra in this place.
　　Let him be judged.

THOTH: Lo, it is Ani, the scribe.
　　Faithful is he,
　　Long in the fields of the earth
　　Served he the gods.

GODS: Yet must he answer to us.
　　Let him be judged.

ANI: Hail, O ye gods, who judge me,
　　Ye lords of Right and Truth!
　　No theft have I committed,
　　No murder have I done,
　　I have not been deceitful
　　Nor taught my tongue to lie.
　　No man have I assaulted
　　Nor laid his fields in waste.

No heart has learned to fear me,
Nor did I walk in wrath.
No seeds of strife I scattered,
Nor brought I any tears.

GODS: Let the heart of the dead be weighed.
Let the feather of Truth
Measure his heart in the balance.

(*Anubis takes the heart of Ani and places it in the scales against the feather of Truth*)

ANI (*kneeling*): O my heart, my mother,
My heart, my mother,
The source of my being,
Thou spring of existence,
Stand not against me,
Part thou not from me,
Thrust me not back
At the feet of my judges.
May thou come forth
In the light of the morning,
Into the Fields of Peace.

ANUBIS: This heart is truly weighed,
And it is pure.
In righteousness and truth
It hath withstood the Balance.

GODS: Let him come in, and safely dwell
Amid the Fields of Peace.
Let not the jaws of Death devour
The soul that overcometh.

(*Horus takes Ani by the hand and leads him to Osiris*)

HORUS: I bring to thee, Osiris,
This spirit-traveller,
The dust of earthly evil
New-shaken from his feet.
His deeds have been adjudged,
His heart is truly weighed,

> O grant him now thy welcome,
> And thy peace.

ANI: Behold, O lord of lords,
> I stand, a living soul,
> Sinless before thy throne I come,
> To gaze upon Osiris.
> Make me thy son, O let me be
> Beloved of thee for ever.

(*Osiris raises his hand*)

ANI (*stepping towards front of stage*):
> Now shall I dwell in the heavens,
> Death overpassed,
> The terror and dark of the Underworld,
> Fled is the night . . .
> Dim are the judgments of men.
> Ra is the light.

CURTAIN

THE RETURN OF ODYSSEUS

(age 10–11)

No comment is necessary on this well-known story. It would be advisable, however, for the children performing the play to hear something of the previous adventures of the hero, as well as the details of the events which took place between his actual arrival on the shores of Ithaca and his first entry into his own hall. This play is suited to the more mature of this age-group—for eleven-year-olds rather than ten.

PROLOGUE

THE SEA-SHORE

Athene, and Odysseus (lying asleep)

ATHENE: Arise, Odysseus, shake the cloak
    Of downy sleep that wraps thee round,
    Behold the homeland of thy folk,
    Thy feet once more on goodly ground.
    Know'st thou not Ithaca, thy land—
    Nor her who doth before thee stand?

ODYSSEUS: Great goddess—nay, I knew thee not,
    Nor yet the shore whereon I lay . . .
    O wise Athene, since thou brought
    Us victory in the Trojan fray,
    Thou hast not succoured me in aught,
    Nor looked upon my stricken way.
    Ten years I wandered from my realm,
    My ship, my company, are gone;
    Nor stood thou once beside my helm,
    But strangers left me here, alone.

ATHENE: Ne'er did I doubt thy safe return,
    And now, thy trials all but done,
    Here am I come that thou may learn

Tidings of thy wife and son.
Penelope sits in sorrow's thrall,
Weeping the empty hours away,
While shameless suitors throng thy hall
Wasting thy substance, till the day
When she, despairing of thy life,
Shall give herself to one as wife.
Thy son, Telemachus, is grown
Comely and tall, to man's estate;
Sturdy of limb is he, and one
Shall help thee crown the wooers' fate.

ODYSSEUS: Come, grey-eyed goddess, do thou weave
Some counsel wise whereby my hand
May work their ruin, and achieve
The will of Zeus. And if thou stand
Beside me as in days of old
And make my spirit clear and bold,
Then let my foes three hundred be,
I'll conquer, if thou succour me.

ATHENE: Fear not, for I shall be thy guide.
But come, I shall disguise thy frame,
Make waste thy skin, thy hair beside,
That none may know thee, nor thy name.
Thine eyes grow dim, thy features grey,
In foulest garments make thy way—
Till, shameless in their vaunted power,
Thy foes shall meet their fated hour.

SCENE I

HALL OF ODYSSEUS

(*Wooers seated, feasting, attended by servants. Telemachus seated apart*)

CHORUS OF WOOERS:
Come, fill the platter, pour the wine,
Here shall we sit, nor think to part

    Until Penelope divine
    Shall yield her gracious heart.

EURYMACHUS (*1st Wooer*):
    That will not be until the shroud
    She daily weaves with anxious care
    Shall be completed. She has vowed
    That then she will her choice declare.

3RD WOOER: Surely that tale no man believes,
    For by each setting of the sun
    The prudent Penelope unweaves
    What all day long her hands have done.

4TH WOOER: There sits Telemachus—alone,
    Nor thinks he e'er to end this strife
    And move his mother's heart of stone
    To give herself to wife.

TELEMACHUS: Ye who devour my father's store
    Of wine and cattle, goats and sheep,
    Think ye that I from out this door
    Should thrust my mother forth, and reap
    The vengeance of the gods that should
    Fall on my ingratitude?
    Nay, if in aught ye are displeased,
    Quit ye my halls and seek your own.
    There let ye feast and be appeased,
    And eat the corn yourselves have sown.
    But if ye deem that such a use
    Of one man's goods is fair and fit,
    Then will I call on mighty Zeus
    That ye may perish where ye sit!

        (*Wooers laugh: Enter Odysseus*)

5TH WOOER: "Then will I call on mighty Zeus!"

6TH WOOER: "That ye may perish where ye sit!"

TELEMACHUS (*to servant*):
    Here stands a stranger at our door.
    Give him of bread and flesh to eat,

    And should his hunger crave for more,
    Then bid him beg the wooers' meat.

ODYSSEUS: Fair youth, may all the gods conspire
    To send thee soon thy heart's desire!

(Enter Minstrel with lyre, and sings)

(Athene appears in background, touches Odysseus: and passes on)

ODYSSEUS (*Rising and approaching wooers*):
    Fair sirs, your pity now I crave,
    A homeless wanderer am I,
    Thrust by Poseidon's thundering wave
    Upon an alien shore to lie.

(He goes to each of the wooers, and receives food)

7TH WOOER: Who is this man, of lot so hard?

8TH WOOER: So dim of eye and weather-scarred.

9TH WOOER: Some prowling beggar, I'll be bound.

10TH WOOER: Rubbing our doorposts smooth and round!

ANTINOUS (*2nd Wooer*):
    What knave hath brought this idle rough?
    Need we such kill-joys at our feast?
    Have we not beggars here enough?

ODYSSEUS: Friend, give me somewhat—even the least
    Of thy rich portion, for thou art
    Like to a king who should impart
    Bounty to all, both man and beast.
    For I too once owned house and hall
    Where never wanderer begged in vain;
    But Zeus in wrath hath taken all
    And cast me forth in dearth and pain.
    Far have I roamed in sore distress,
    And know no lot but bitterness.

ANTINOUS: What god hath sent this plaguey pest
    To vex us with his din and babble?

Stand back, thou thrice-unwelcome guest,—
Keep thy foul fingers from my table!

ODYSSEUS: Lo, now I see, with all thy grace,
Thou hast not wit to match thy face,
Nor yet the heart to proffer free
The bread another gave to thee.

ANTINOUS: Rail not at me, thou idle thrall,
Nor utter here these scornful tones,
Lest we should drag thee through the hall
And strip thy flesh from off thy bones.
Begone!
(He strikes Odysseus with a stool)

EURYMACHUS: Antinous, thou dost ill to smite
The hapless wanderer in his need.
Doomed man art thou, in heaven's sight,
If there be gods indeed.

3RD WOOER: Yea, and the gods are wont to take
The shape of strangers now and then,
And through the land their journeys make
To watch the deeds of men.

ANTINOUS: Teach me not how I should behave!
This man is but a lying slave.

(Enter Penelope, with maidens)

PENELOPE: Telemachus, what deeds of shame
Are done beneath the eye of heaven,
That strangers sheltering in thy name
Dishonoured from thy halls are driven!

TELEMACHUS: Thine anger, mother mine, is just.
These men unseat my will, and thrust
Their evil on me. So I do
Not what I will, but what I must.

EURYMACHUS: Penelope, most wise and fair,
If all Achaeans in the land
Could see thee as thou standest there,
Countless they'd be who'd seek thy hand!

PENELOPE: Eurymachus, when long ago
　　　　Odysseus my lord went hence
　　　　To fatal Troy, I surely know
　　　　The gods destroyed my excellence.
　　　　Well I remember on that day
　　　　Odysseus took me by the hand
　　　　"Lady, not all will find their way
　　　　Home safely to their native land;
　　　　For Trojans, too, they say, are brave
　　　　And skilled in arms—so have a care
　　　　For all things that are mine, and save
　　　　Till manhood's strength, my son and heir.
　　　　Then marry whom thou wilt, and leave
　　　　Thy house, nor turn aside to grieve."
　　　　So spake he, and the gods now send
　　　　The day when these things have an end.
　　　　Tomorrow shall your skill and strength
　　　　Decide whom I must wed at length.
　　　　To string the bow Odysseus drew
　　　　Shall each one strive, then straightway through
　　　　Twelve axes in a careful line
　　　　Shall each one shoot an arrow fine.
　　　　Then he who first fulfils the task
　　　　Shall win the prize. I only ask
　　　　That now ye leave this hall and bide
　　　　Until tomorrow's eventide.

ANTINOUS: Lady, with joy thou fill'st our hearts.
　　　　Gladly we take the proffered odds,
　　　　And thankfully, e'er each departs,
　　　　Pour a libation to the gods.

ALL: And now may heaven send us grace
　　　To win so wonderful a face!

(They begin to leave the hall)

3RD WOOER: Two-fold the task—both arm and eye
　　　　Must show their rightful sovereignty.

4TH WOOER: Aye, but the arm must venture first . . .

5TH WOOER: This show of strength is not the worst . . .

5TH WOOER: Mine arm might rival Hercules!

(Exeunt, laughing and talking)

PENELOPE: Poor wanderer, only thou art left!
    Hast thou no place to lay thy head?

ODYSSEUS: Lady, of all I am bereft,
    My house, my family, my bed.

PENELOPE: Come, sit by me and quickly say
    If aught of Odysseus thou canst tell . . .
    Didst hear of him upon thy way?

ODYSSEUS: Lady, I knew him well.

PENELOPE: Then tell me, stranger, whence thou art,
    Thy lineage, thy land, thy race.
    Thy words more strangely stir my heart
    Of any who have sought this place.

ODYSSEUS: Toward the noonday sun there lies
    A land amid the wine-dark sea,
    Where rich and fair the cities rise
    O'er water surging endlessly.
    There was I prince, and thither came
    With beaked ships Troy-ward battling sore
    Odysseus of mighty name,
    Borne by the winds upon our shore.
    Then did I lead him to my house
    And goodly entertainment gave
    Until the angry gods who rouse
    Relentless winds, did soothe the wave.
    And so upon a smiling day
    They lifted anchor—and away.

PENELOPE: O how thy words do tug my heart!
    Yet would I try thee, friend as thou art.
    If thou didst truly entertain
    My lord with all his godlike train,
    Tell me, that day he sought thy shore,
    What raiment then Odysseus wore.

ODYSSEUS: Lady, 'tis hard, from long ago
   To recollect,—but this I know;
   A purple cloak he wore, two-fold,
   And fastened with a brooch of gold
   Whereon was marvellously drawn
   A hound which held a dappled fawn.
   The doublet that he had was one
   So smooth, it glistened as the sun . . .
   And with him was a henchman tall,
   Brown-skinned and curly-haired, of all
   His company, he deemed him best,—
   Eurybates . . .

PENELOPE: O stranger guest,
   Thou speakest true. That very cloak
   I gave my lord the day I spoke
   My last farewell, while in its fold
   I pinned that very brooch of gold.
   Alas, he will return no more
   Homeward to his native shore.

ODYSSEUS: Nay, lady, weep not—by my word,
   I'll tell thee all that I have heard—
   Odysseus is nigh at hand
   And yet alive, in friendly land,
   And with him such a treasure brings
   As is the heritage of kings.
   Lady, he'll come! so have I sworn,—
   As the old moon wanes and the new is born.

PENELOPE: Ah, stranger, would that this could be!
   My heart speaks otherwise to me . . .
   Come, handmaids, wash this stranger's feet,
   And bring him bed and blankets meet,
   Which soft and warm he may lie on
   Until the golden-thronéd dawn.

ODYSSEUS: Wife of revered Odysseus,—nay.
   Such things I long have put away,
   And since I journeyed forth alone
   I gladly lie on earth or stone.

Baths for the feet no more I crave,
Nor yet shall any youthful slave
Touch foot of mine, unless there be
Some old wife, true of heart, and she
Hath known the troubles I have known.

PENELOPE: Yea, one I have to fit this part,
Old, and of understanding heart,
She that did nurse my lord forlorn
From the first hour that he was born.
Come, Eurycleia, wash this man
Nor shrink his faded limbs to scan.
So may Odysseus at this hour
Be weak of frame, bereft of power.

EURYCLEIA: Glad will I do what thou dost ask . . .
For pity urgeth to the task.
But mark the word that I shall say—
Of all the strangers to this day
None was so like my master sweet,
As thou in fashion, voice and feet.

ODYSSEUS: True—even so do men exclaim
How like we are in face and frame,
And . . . surely, thou dost mark the same.

(A slave brings a basin of water)

EURYCLEIA *(to Odysseus)*:
Well I remember, when, full-grown,
He faced a raging boar alone,
With eager spear to thrust him through—
Too quick the monster sideways drew—
Struck with his furious tusk, and far
Did plough his flesh . . .
     Here is the scar!
My child, Odysseus, thou art he!

ODYSSEUS *(to Eurycleia)*:
Hush! woman, wouldst thou ruin me
And see me utterly destroyed?

> Hold fast thy tongue if thou'd avoid
> Thine own swift death, and silent be!

(*to Penelope*): Lady, I thank thee for thy care
> And now to rest I would repair
> For weary are the limbs of one
> Who daily wandereth with the sun.

PENELOPE: Stranger, I bid thee now good-night
> For nearly dawns the dreaded day
> When by a lonely arrow's flight
> I needs must sell myself away.

ODYSSEUS: Lady, let not thy heart despair.
> Odysseus will himself be there.

(*Odysseus lies down to sleep as Penelope and her maidens pass out*)

(*Enter two handmaids on their way into the town. They start back in disgust on seeing Odysseus*)

1ST HANDMAID: A plague upon thee, idle wretch!
> Is't not enough that we should fetch
> Thy supper to thee? Must thou lie
> Here all night long, to peep and spy?

2ND HANDMAID: Who cares what he may see? Not I!

(*Exeunt, laughing*)

(*Enter Athene*)

ATHENE: Odysseus, let doubting have no part
> In the counsels of thy heart.
> I am thy stay, thy guide, thy friend.
> I shall preserve thee to the end.

CURTAIN

SCENE II

(Wooers seated at table, Telemachus and Odysseus apart. 10th Wooer struggles to string bow, as Penelope stands at back of stage, watching)

9TH WOOER: Nay, thou hast failed. Give me the bow!

(seizes it, and tries)

8TH WOOER: Thou lackest strength to bend it so,—
To span an interval so wide—

(he tries)

(Wooers laugh)

7TH WOOER: Mine is the trial—stand aside!

(he tries)

6TH WOOER: No hope hast thou to win the prize!

(he tries)

5TH WOOER: See how his lordly muscles rise!
Yet never nearer moves the string.
Of *me* shall all the minstrels sing!
Give *me* the bow!

(he tries)

ODYSSEUS: My lords, I pray
You leave this contest for today
And yield to me the polished bow
That, making trial, I may know
If after wandering, at length
My limbs have lost their supple strength.

ANTINOUS: Thou wretched man, hast thou no wit?
Art not contented there to sit
And share our banquet in this hall,
But must arrange our lives withal?
Art thou so impudent to be
A suitor for Penelope?

TELEMACHUS: He is no suitor for her hand,
  Nor need he be: but understand
  That in my father's house I know
  I'm master. (*To servant*) Bring this man the bow!

  (*Servant takes up bow*)

WOOERS: Thou vagabond! thou wretched slave!
  Wouldst thou go swiftly to thy grave?
  Set down thy master's bow, nor bring
  Dishonour on a sacred thing.

  (*Servant sets down bow in fright*)

TELEMACHUS: Eumaeus, I am thy master's son.
  Let what I have ordained be done.

(*Odysseus takes the bow and examines it*)

4TH WOOER: In truth, he hath a knowing eye!

3RD WOOER: As if some flaw he would espy!

EURYMACHUS: Perchance he makes one, and would know
  How best the cunning shape should go.

  (*Odysseus lightly strings the bow and twangs the cord. Sound of thunder, while Athene appears in doorway*)

ODYSSEUS (*to Telemachus*): In nowise have I done thee shame,
  Nor shall I miss the intended mark—
  My friends, Odysseus is my name!

(*throwing off rags*): On with the banquet, lest the dark
  Should mar the pleasure of our game!
  Let music crown this happy chance.
  Now may we see the wooers dance!

  (*The Wooers are panic-stricken, rush to hide behind chairs and tables, but Odysseus shoots them, one by one*)

  Ye dogs, in your false hearts ye said
  I never more should homeward turn,
  And thus ye took my meat and bread,
  Nor thought your own to earn.

And while I yet was full in life
Ye traitorously wooed my wife.
Ye had no fear of gods or men,
But wasted freely house and hall.
How little did ye picture then
The bands of death were on you all!

(*Penelope approaches with outstretched arms*)

CURTAIN

ROMULUS AND REMUS

(age 11–12)

In this little play, written for a small group of children, an attempt is made to sketch, in three brief episodes, the early story of the fabled founders of Rome. Faustulus, a shepherd in the service of Amulius, King of Alba Longa, is sent by his wife Laurentia one evening to gather faggots, when he discovers the two babes by the river-side. He brings them to his cottage where the childless couple gladly adopt them as their own. One stormy evening some nine years later a shepherd, taking shelter in their cottage, tells the tale of how he, on a night similar to this, had been given the task by King Amulius—who had usurped the throne of his brother Numitor—to drown Numitor's twin grandsons in the river. The suspicions of the couple, who had begun to think that these were no ordinary children, are now confirmed, but, fearing the King, they say nothing. In the third scene the boys are now grown up and follow their foster-father's calling as shepherds to Amulius. Strife has broken out between the shepherds of Amulius and of his deposed brother Numitor, and the young Remus has been captured and brought before Numitor who, struck by the young man's appearance, begins to question him as to his origin when a riot breaks out against Amulius, and Faustulus rushes in, accompanied by Romulus, to tell the whole story. They urge Numitor to seize his rightful throne, aided by the two young men, but Numitor, now an old man, offers the kingship to his grandsons. Romulus, however, declares their intention to build a new city—the future Rome. They go out to meet the crowds, and Faustulus is left alone. He sees in all this the finger of the gods, and he has a vision of the future of this new city, its early grandeur, its decline, and at length to his horror the picture of incense burning on an altar in honour of a mere man—(the later Caesars)—instead of to a god. Finally he sees something which he cannot yet understand—"three crosses on a silent hill".

SCENE I

The Finding of the Babes

An Open Place. Evening

FAUSTULUS *(shivering)*:
    The wind blows comfortless and cold,
    The clouds do battle overhead,

The sun has lost his kindly gold
And sinks in stormy red.
May all the gods have pity on
The soul that has no bed!
Aye—sticks, she said—some timber dry
To keep our hearth alive and bright—
There's need to hasten, for the sky
Is shadowed by the wings of night,
And fiercely dark the river rolls,
Ruthless in its might.
The river—aye—it well may be
That, floating on its bosom brown,
Some branches of a broken tree
Or basket drifting from the town
Have caught upon a reedy bank
As they went swiftly down.
     (*Exit*)
    (*Enter Laurentia*)

LAURENTIA: Come, haste, the fire is all but out,
 And supper's cooling in the pan!
 Ah, there you have a bundle stout—
 Some goodly faggots. Hasten, man—
 What ails you that you walk so slow?
 Weighs the wood upon you so?

FAUSTULUS (*enters*): Good wife, strange faggots have I got
 Which ne'er will turn the embers red,
 Nor save our cooling supper-pot—
 But warm your heart instead!
 See what lay dry upon the bank
 Where late the flooded river sank!

LAURENTIA: Poor things, their hands are cold as clay,
 Their clothes all spotted by the mire,—
 Their spark of life has died away. . . .

FAUSTULUS: Good wife, go lay them by the fire. . . .
 The gods have work for us to do. . . .
 And I'll go gathering anew.
     (*Exit Laurentia*)

What may these happenings portend?
A new beginning, or an end?
Strange signs accompanied my quest—
Six vultures winging to the west,
A peal of thunder rolling wild,
A she-wolf mothering a child!
The gods are husbanding their ways,
And sow the seeds of mighty days.

(Exit)

SCENE II

The Visitor

In Faustulus' Cottage

(Faustulus at fire, Laurentia listening at bedroom door)

LAURENTIA: They're quiet now—their breathing deep
Betokens the approach of sleep.

FAUSTULUS: The day has rung with merriment . . .
From dawn to sunset they have spent
Their hours among the sheep. They played
At shepherds. They were wolves. They strayed
Beyond tomorrow and became
Warriors of mighty name,
Waving willow-swords that flank
The unoffending river-bank.

LAURENTIA: 'Tis plain no shepherd's sons are they,
Their blood is nobler than they know.
For I have seen how, in their play,
They rule the other children so.

FAUSTULUS: They are a gift the gods have sent.
We had no children of our own.
'Twere better to abide content

And leave such thoughts alone.
Hark, how the wind in fury flies!
There's busy doing in the skies.

(*Knock. Enter Shepherd*)

SHEPHERD: I saw your cabin light afar,
Twinkling like a lonely star.
The night is wild upon the hill . . .

FAUSTULUS: Enter, friend, and take your fill
Of warmth and talk and simple fare,
And aught of good I have to share.

SHEPHERD: I have to wend me to the town
Before the darkness closes down . . .
But let me share your hearth awhile
To cheer me on the latest mile.
The clouds are hounded by the blast,
And now the river rises fast
Beyond the bridge's topmost beam
And trees are standing in the stream . . .
I have not seen it flooded so
Not since nine long years ago.

FAUSTULUS: Nine years ago, you think it was?

SHEPHERD: Well I remember it—because
I had to do a certain thing
For Amulius, the king.

FAUSTULUS: You are his shepherd?

SHEPHERD: Aye, 'tis true—
No shepherd's task I had to do.
The times were wild and troublous grown,
The king had seized his brother's throne,
And, fearful lest he lose his crown,
Gave me two royal babes to drown!

FAUSTULUS: To *drown*?

SHEPHERD: Like rats,—poor helpless things!
And so I took the baby kings

And floated them upon the deep
In their cradle, fast asleep.
The hungry river clutched his prey
And swiftly swept the bark away.
I have not seen so fierce a flow—
Not since nine long years ago.

LAURENTIA (*excited*): Good man, good man, I told you so!

FAUSTULUS (*trying to cover her remark*):
My wife, indeed, remembers well
The river-flood of which you tell . . .
The fire needs faggots. Draw your chair.
You have a goodly way to fare . . .

SHEPHERD: Not far, and yet I must away
While glimmers the departing day.
I thank you for your friendly cheer—
I'm warmer now . . .

                (*Exit*)

FAUSTULUS: The storm, I fear
Is blowing fiercer than before . . .
Dark danger's standing at our door!
The king will put the boys to death—
And you and me—if any breath
Of this be whispered in his ear.

LAURENTIA: Come, Faustulus, there's nought to fear . . .
The gods will have us in their keeping . . .
Come—see our little princes sleeping!

                (*Exeunt*)

SCENE III

The Captive

The House of Numitor. Eleven Years Later

(Numitor, Servant and Remus)

NUMITOR: Leave him to me! Let loose his hands!

(Exit Servant)

    Whence come you? Of those lawless bands
    That steal my cattle, rob my lands?

REMUS: No thief am I—but such a one
    As tends the sheep—a shepherd's son,
    Yet well I know to hunt and slay
    Both wolf and robber.

NUMITOR: And you say
    That you are not the chief of those
    Who make themselves my servants' foes?

REMUS: We are their foes for reason plain—
    We did but carry back again
    The cattle they did steal from us,
    The servants of Amulius.

NUMITOR: A servant, say you? Nay, I deem
    That you are nobler than you seem.
    Come, tell me of your name and birth!

REMUS: My name is Remus. Little worth
    Is my condition—yet of old
    A strange and fateful tale is told.
    Our foster-father saw us lie—
    My brother Romulus and I—
    Two babes within one cradle wrapped,
    Where late the flooded river lapped,
    And here a she-wolf, heaven-sent

Gave us kindly nourishment.
But of our birth I nothing know.

NUMITOR: That was—how many years ago?

REMUS: Some twenty years.

NUMITOR: That was a time
Of darkness, death and royal crime.
Amulius from my daughter tore
Unpitying the babes she bore—
The children of the god of war.

(Shouting off)

Are you her child?

(Enter Faustulus and Romulus)

FAUSTULUS: My lord, I pray,
Listen to the words I say!
This is no shepherd's son, nor he,
His brother, who awaits with me
To do your will. These noble ones
Are indeed your daughter's sons.
Long years did I withhold this thing
Fearing the vengeance of the king.
But now to Romulus I've told
His fateful story—and behold
Your grandson with a mighty band
Cries vengeance, and his eager hand
Awaits your bidding. Fire and sword
Shall sweep the city at your word.
The king sits trembling and alone.
Arise and seize your rightful throne!

NUMITOR: Nay—I am old—'twere better now
To crown a brave and youthful brow.

ROMULUS: 'Tis not for youth to sit him down
Contented with an easy crown.
For us the task to build anew
Where yet the early morning dew

Knows not the feet of man.—Our will
To set a city on a hill,
A little town, where all may be
Unburdened, bountiful and free.—
Come, for the time awaits us . . .

  (*Exeunt Numitor, Romulus and Remus. Shouts off*)

FAUSTULUS: Now moves the finger of the gods
  Where groping man slow-footed trods.
  My little task is all but done,
  Yet far beyond the setting sun
  In cloudy pictures I behold—
  Built of the crimson and the gold—
  A many-pillared city rise,
  Whose domes and arches paint the skies.
  The tramp of marching feet I hear,
  The victor's shout, the clash of spear,
  And shepherds in the farthest lands
  Hearken to her stern commands.
  But now with horror comes apace
  Darkness on the city's face,
  And incense smoking on a stone
  To a man upon a throne.
  The shadows deepen, faith is not,
  The truth forsaken, gods forgot . . .
  And far—upon an evening still—
  Three crosses on a silent hill . . .

      Finis

THE EMPEROR'S VISION

(age 11-12)

This is not so much a play in itself as a prologue to a Christmas play. The story is taken from Selma Lagerlöf's book of Legends already mentioned. On the night of the birth of Jesus, Augustus Caesar, with friends and slaves, climbs the Capitoline Hill in Rome to offer a sacrifice to Jupiter and to see if by some sign the god approves of the building here of a temple in honour of Caesar himself as a god. His flattering friends assure him—in spite of the sacrificial dove having escaped from his hands—that this is surely the place, and that the utter silence of all Nature at this moment is a sign of Jupiter's approval. Suddenly a strange figure in the background who all this time has been gazing eastwards, begins to speak. She is an ancient Sybil, and she sees in a vision the shepherds, the angels and the star. But Augustus and his friends pay little heed, and just as his followers hail him as god of Rome, the Sybil turns to him in scorn and points him to the vision of a very different event.

This story, which places the materialistic outlook of Rome so dramatically beside the birth of Christianity, shows at the same moment a man aspiring to become a god, and the God who is about to become a man.

SCENE

THE CAPITOL HILL, ROME

The Sybil standing, gazing eastward, her back only being seen

(Enter two Torchbearers)

1ST TORCHBEARER:
How dark the night is! There's no eye
In all the heavens, and the gods
Have turned their faces from the earth.
This lonely flame doth carve for us
The hollow space in which we stand.
All else is bedded in the dark.

2ND TORCHBEARER:
An ocean seems to weigh us down,

And we, like crabs, do crawl upon
The sightless flooring of the sea.
I would I were in bed. This hour
Is not for honest men, nor yet
For emperors to be abroad.
Why doth Augustus sacrifice
At such a time and place?

1ST TORCHBEARER: To seek the will of Jupiter
If here a temple may be built
To Caesar, as a god.

2ND TORCHBEARER: Are there
Not gods enough, and temples too?

1ST TORCHBEARER:
One more we need—a god of flesh—
To rule the Roman world, and give
Peace to her people, justice, power,
And plenteousness of bread and wine.
And such a god is Caesar.

AUGUSTUS (*off*): Set down the litter. I shall walk
From here to the appointed place.

(*Enter Augustus and friends, followed by slaves*)

Is it the hour of night that brings
Such stillness to the air? It seems
All nature lies in sleep, or stands,
Finger on lip, awaiting day.

1ST FRIEND: There is no voice in all the earth.
The trees are silent, and the hills
Withhold their streams. The Tiber's self
Is motionless . . . Hark ye! . . . No sound.

2ND FRIEND: 'Tis an auspicious hour! The world
Does reverence to Caesar. See!
The very torches flicker dim!
And yonder tree bows down.

3RD FRIEND: Is that
    A tree? Methinks a thing of stone—
    A statue from the Capitol
    Hath wandered here on fleshless feet.
    O Sire, what omen's this?

1ST FRIEND: No statue,—but a woman. See,
    She lifts her head, as she would speak.
    It is the sibyl—agèd one,
    Whose years are countless—she who writes
    Dark prophecies on withered leaves
    And floats them on the wind. . . .
    What can *she* seek on such a night?

2ND FRIEND: She comes to honour Caesar! Quick,
    Let us bring forth the sacrifice.
    The gods are waiting and the hour
    Is rich with goodly promise.

            (*The altar is set up by the slaves*)

AUGUSTUS: Bring me the dove; prepare the fire . . .
    Alas!—the bird has slipped my grasp
    And taken wing into the night.
    This bodes no good.

2ND FRIEND: Perchance the dove
    Hath sped direct to Jupiter!

SIBYL (*speaking as in a trance*):
    There are sheep which gently pass
    Fearless o'er the starlit grass.
    There are shepherds wrapped in sleep
    Careless of the wandering sheep.
    Beasts of prey with quiet eyes
    Rest where sheep or shepherd lies,
    All is peace, the woods are still,
    Hushed the winds about the hill.

AUGUSTUS: What saith she? Doth she prophesy?

3RD FRIEND: Perchance 'twas she, with cunning art,
    Who snatched the dove from out thy hand.

SIBYL: Earth's midnight hour has come. Behold,
　　The flash of wings above the fold!
　　The air is filled with song, and far
　　To eastward flames a star . . .

AUGUSTUS: See—all things quicken, nature stirs
　　As in a happy dream. The air
　　Blows softly, and the curtained dark
　　Is lifted from the earth.

2ND FRIEND:　　　　　　　It is
　　A sign, O Caesar, from the gods,
　　And nature greets thee as her king.
　　To thee a temple shall be raised
　　And men shall worship on this hill
　　Caesar Augustus, god of Rome.

ALL *(kneeling)*: Hail, Caesar, god of Rome!

SIBYL *(suddenly turning to face Caesar)*:
　　Fools! ye know not what ye say,
　　And darkness shrouds your souls.
　　Your eyes are sightless, and your ears
　　Are stopped with mortal pride. Come,
　　Caesar Augustus, lord of earth,
　　And look upon the Light! Behold,
　　The veil is lifted. See afar
　　A hill where sheep and shepherds are. . . .

　　　　　　(Scene of Shepherds opens)

DOROTHEA

(age 11-12)

This play is taken from the legend of St. Dorothea, yet it is history in the sense that it gives a picture of the trials and sufferings of the Christians during the Roman persecutions. It is a very beautiful story, suitable for children of 12 rather than 11, for certain passages demand some genuine emotion during the trial scene. The second scene, by contrast, requires a quiet restraint. It will be seen that a good "Theophilus" is essential.

SCENE I

A Law Court in Caesarea, A.D. 303.
Seated at a table is Theophilus, a young lawyer, writing.
Enter a Slave, bearing a tripod for sacrifice.

SLAVE: Where should the altar stand, Theophilus?

THEOPHILUS *(without looking up)*:
　There by the chair. When comes the Governor?

SLAVE: At the third hour, for there is much
　That lieth to his hand.

THEOPHILUS:　　　　　Most true.
　Bring me some word of his approach.

(Exit Slave)

(Enter Antoninus, a pleasure-loving young nobleman)

ANTONINUS: Ho, Theophilus—art gleaning still
　New victims for the hungry sword?
　Come—dine with me—for Priscus comes,
　Sempronius,—my choicest friends,—
　And lose awhile among the stars
　These dusty parchments of the day.

THEOPHILUS: If then my wings will carry me . . .

ANTONINUS: What—is the task so wearisome?

THEOPHILUS (*with sudden anger*):
    It is the Christians, Antony,
    Who honour not the gods, and bring
    Disaster on our Roman lands.
    This impious superstition grows
    And fattens like a poisonous plant
    In some barbarian swamp.

ANTONINUS: They come for trial here?

THEOPHILUS (*wearily*):   All day!

ANTONINUS: My poor Theophilus! . . . Farewell.
    I'll to the baths, and then to dine.
    A couch awaits thee,—fail me not . . .

(*He turns to go with a wave of the hand, and meets Sempronius, who enters hurriedly and importantly*)

ANTONINUS: Well met, Sempronius! Why such haste?
    Art come for trial?—or to beg
    A word from good Theophilus?
    He's short of words as thou of breath.

SEMPRONIUS: Nay, I but bring the final roll
    Of those that have been gathered in,—
    A goodly number, young and old,
    And one, they say, both young and fair,
    Too fair to live, too young to die.

THEOPHILUS: A maiden?

SEMPRONIUS: Aye, gentle and good,
    Well known as Dorothea. She—
    Her childhood scarcely left behind—
    Is thick entangled with the fancies
    Of her most obstinate sect.

THEOPHILUS (*musingly and scarcely addressing his friends*):
    I knew a maid of such a name,

Some summers past I spoke to her,
One golden evening as I rode
Beside a garden wall.
So light she moved among her flowers
You would have thought she blossomed there
And, loosened from her earthly place,
Now hovered with the wind.
Then laughingly I begged a flower,
A rose, I said,—a bud or two,—
And gaily upward shone her face
So trustingly to mine.
She gave me roses—red, she said,
For reason I have since forgot,—
And apples of a golden hue,
And with a merry laugh she ran
And hid among the leaves.

ANTONINUS: How rapt our friend is in his thoughts!

SEMPRONIUS: Speak to her then, if this be she . . .

(*Noise of crowd off. Enter crowd, come to witness trials, talking and laughing. Exeunt Antoninus and Sempronius. Enter Slave.*)

SLAVE: Pray, silence for the Governor!

(*Enter Sapricius, the Governor. He takes his seat*)

SAPRICIUS: Bring forth the prisoners.

(*Enter guards, with two young women*)

                        Who is first,
And what the accusation?

THEOPHILUS (*rising and reading*): "Fulvia, a freedwoman, has confessed herself a Christian and an enemy of the immortal gods."

SAPRICIUS (*kindly*): Thou knowest the Emperor's decree
That all must sacrifice to him.
Here stands an altar; do thou scatter
Incense on the holy flame.

FULVIA: I may not, for our Lord forbids
That we should worship idols . . .

SAPRICIUS: Then, must we try *persuasion*? See
   In yonder room an iron bed
   Above a slowly-heating fire,
   Prepared for those who disobey.
   Wouldst suffer thus,—or sacrifice?
   Come, 'tis not much we ask of thee.

   (*Fulvia looks, and shudders. She struggles in her soul. But her courage fails her*)

FULVIA: I will do what you ask of me . . .

   (*She approaches the altar and scatters incense*)

THE CROWD (*jubilant*):
   Fulvia has sacrificed! Fulvia has sacrificed!

SAPRICIUS: Fulvia acclaims the gods.
   Let her go free.

   (*Fulvia covers her face with her hands and rushes weeping from the room*)

                    And who art thou?

DOROTHEA: The daughter of a citizen.
   Dorothea is my name.

SAPRICIUS (*casually*): Honour, then, the Roman gods,
   And scatter incense on the flame.

DOROTHEA (*quietly*): I cannot serve such gods as these.

SAPRICIUS: It is the Emperor's command.

DOROTHEA: He may command my body
   But my soul he cannot rule.

SAPRICIUS: These are idle words. Come, girl,
   Trifle not with us, but obey . . .
   See, thou art young and fair. Thy life
   Lies all before thee, golden-clad.
   'Tis not for thee so soon to tread
   The dismal pain-wracked path of death.

DOROTHEA: I fear not death, nor would I choose
   A thousand years of earthly joys—

If thou couldst offer them—in place
Of seeing Him for whom I die.

SAPRICIUS: And who is he thou lov'st so well?

DOROTHEA: He is the Christ, the Son of God.
He hath made light the way of death,
Unlocked for us a garden fair,
The garden of His Paradise.
There grow the roses of the soul,
That blossom red in hearts of gold,
And apples hang from Wisdom's tree
Tasting no more of sin and death. . . .
Noble Sapricius, I pray,
That thou too seek the Way of Life,
And strive with us to enter in
Where all the paths are peace. . . .

SAPRICIUS: This is but madness! Once again,
I bid thee sacrifice. Come, child,
Obey the Emperor's command.
What? thou art stubborn? Then prepare
To meet what now awaits thee . . .

THEOPHILUS (*who has at once recognised Dorothea as the child he had spoken to in the garden, and who has been following everything with increasing interest and emotion, rises at this critical juncture*):
Most noble Sapricius, in thy court
Are two whose counsel might be sought
To help this maid. They have forsworn
Their false beliefs, and cling no more
To Christian superstitions. Grant
That she be given to their care
And learn from older, wiser minds.

SAPRICIUS: Christina, Callista, come forth!

(*Two ladies of the court come forward*)

SAPRICIUS: Ye who were Christians and who now
Have seen the folly of your ways,
Take ye this maid and speak with her.

Then I shall question her again
If haply she should learn of you.

(*Christina and Callista lead Dorothea out*)

Next prisoner!

(*Curtain is lowered for a moment, to denote lapse of some hours*)

SAPRICIUS (*wearily*): Is that the last of all the names?
Then bring the maiden, Dorothea.
Let us question her again.

(*Enter Dorothea with Christina and Callista*)

Ye have spoken to this maiden?

CHRISTINA: We have spoken.

SAPRICIUS: Is she now
Of a wiser frame of mind?

CHRISTINA: We are now all of one mind.

THEOPHILUS (*unable to contain his joy*):
The gods be praised!

SAPRICIUS: Then lead her forth
And let her sacrifice with you.

CHRISTINA (*quietly, but with rising intensity*):
Yea, we will sacrifice,—all three—
And two shall bring such stricken hearts
As ne'er were laid on altar. See,
Sapricius, as we spoke, our hearts
Awoke to music long forgot,
And words resounded in our ears
That spoke of mercy. Those who fall
Or stumble by the way, may rise,
And one lost sheep among the fold
Is sought till she be found. And we—
Lost sheep in blackest night—have found
The morning pathway to the fold,
And we will sacrifice our lives
For Him who led the way.

SAPRICIUS: What mean these words? Why do ye speak
   Of sacrifice of lives?

CHRISTINA (*approaching the altar*): For *thus*,
   Sapricius, we treat your altars!

(*With a sweep of the hand she throws the tripod down*)

SAPRICIUS (*leaps to his feet, beside himself with rage*):
   Sacrilege! Soldiers, seize these women!
   These two—these traitresses—take hence
   And cast them in the boiling cauldron.
   The third—the young one—let her stay
   That she may hear her doom.—Thou,
   Most obstinate and crafty wench,
   With innocent look and subtle tongue,
   Didst creep like snake into their hearts
   And steal away their senses.
   Thou shalt not die so peacefully.
   Ere evening falls thou'lt cry in vain
   For mercy to thy God . . . Go hence—

THEOPHILUS (*in great earnestness, yet scarcely knowing what he is saying*):
   Dorothea—when thou goest
   To the garden of thy God—
   Wilt remember me and send
   A gift of roses from that place?

DOROTHEA: That I will gladly do; farewell.

(*Exit with guards*)

SAPRICIUS (*now recovered from his rage and preparing to leave the court; amused*): That was a clever jest,
   Theophilus,—a *clever* jest!

(*Exit*)

(*But Theophilus hardly hears the remark. He remains where Dorothea left him, gazing in the direction she has gone*)

CURTAIN

SCENE II

Room in Antoninus' House. Theophilus alone, walking up and down, showing the greatest anxiety.

(Enter Sempronius)

SEMPRONIUS: Come, join the feast, Theophilus.
　　Spurn not the kindness of our host.
　　'Tis said the Governor may come,
　　And how imprudent it would be
　　If thou'rt not there to greet him.

THEOPHILUS *(dryly)*: I've seen too much of him today,
　　But if by chance he bring me news,
　　He shall be welcome.
(with emotion)　　　　There is a soul
　　That all day long has suffered torment.
　　I cannot rest until I know
　　It is at peace. . . . Go, ask my pardon
　　Of the company.

(Exit Sempronius)

(From opposite side a child-like angel figure appears, bearing roses)

　　Thou came'st not by the door. Art thou
　　A messenger? Thou bringest tidings.
　　Speak! . . . Yet only smilest thou,
　　Offering me that rosy gift,—
　　Why,—was it not this very gift
　　I begged from Dorothea?—begged
　　In bitterness and doubt of soul,
　　Not knowing such things are.
　　O silent vision!—would mine ears
　　Were half attuned to heavenly sound,
　　Then I might hear thee speak the words
　　That she hath sent me. Yet I know
　　Her soul doth live, and I do praise

And thank the Christ, the Son of God,
Who hath her in His keeping. . . .

(*Enter Antoninus and Sempronius. It is at once evident that they do not see the angel*)

ANTONINUS: Come,
    The Governor is here, and asks
    To speak a word with thee.

SEMPRONIUS: Yes, come,
    For now we learn the maid is dead
    Who so beset thy thoughts,

THEOPHILUS (*quietly*):   I know
    The maid is dead, for she herself
    Hath sent me tidings.

ANTONINUS: Sent thee *tidings*!

THEOPHILUS: And this I also know, my friends,
    That He Whom Christians call their God,
    Is God indeed.

SEMPRONIUS: Speak not such madness!
    Thou who so spent thy time and powers
    To bring these evil-doers to justice,
    Thou who so hated them, and planned
    New ways of torture. . . . Thou art *mad*!

THEOPHILUS: Not mad, Sempronius, but now
    Awakened from a dream. . . . I gave
    No mercy, and I ask for none.
    If there be mercy for my deeds,
    It dwells in heaven, not on earth . . .
    Pray God, I shall not fail, but go
    Unfalteringly down the road
    Made fair by many feet . . .
    Farewell, my friends, and leave me now.
    Pray tell the Governor I am
    His prisoner, and shall attend
    For trial in the morning.

ANTONINUS (*despairingly*):   Theophilus!

THEOPHILUS: No more . . . farewell.

(*Exeunt Sempronius and Antoninus. Theophilus gazes steadily in front of him. The angel approaches*)

SLOW CURTAIN

CORNELIA

THE MOTHER OF THE GRACCHI

(*age 11-12*)

This play deals with incidents in the lives of two Roman reformers, the brothers Gracchi, at the beginning of the second century B.C., and their mother, Cornelia, who devoted her life to the upbringing of her famous sons. The brothers, Tiberius and Gaius, fought in turn to reform the agrarian laws so that the Plebeians might have land; but each was killed at length in the struggle, Tiberius at the age of 30, and Gaius some years later, at 32.

After the first scene, depicting the well-known story of Cornelia and her two young boys, the first part of the play deals with Tiberius up to the point where he addresses the people and threatens to veto every other new law until he gets his way. The second part shows Gaius, having now taken up his dead brother's campaign, preparing for armed revolt against the Senate. Proclaimed a traitor, his few remaining friends fight a desperate rear-guard action in an attempt to save him, but this merely gives him time and opportunity to bring about his own death. The final scene shows how the heroic Cornelia receives the news of the death of her second son in the fight for justice.

As the play depends upon a certain acquaintance with the background of the period, it is perhaps more suited to the history classroom than public performance, unless a brief introduction is first given to the audience.

SCENE I

House of Cornelia. She is seated, telling a story to her two young sons, Tiberius and Gaius. Time: Evening.

CORNELIA: So Brutus spoke in the Forum to the people of Rome and said: "Will you suffer such a tyrant or any of his race to rule longer over you, O Romans?" Then the people arose in wrath and when Tarquin the Proud returned to Rome, the gates of the city were shut against him . . . Thus was banished the last of the kings of Rome.

GAIUS: And did the Romans *fight* him?

CORNELIA: Not then. But he fled to Etruria and from thence he brought a great army against Rome. In that battle, Rome was victorious, but the good and brave Brutus was slain.

GAIUS: Shall I, too, fight for Rome one day?

CORNELIA: Perhaps, my son. But I hope my two sons will fight not only for Rome, but for right and justice, for the poor and the oppressed.

TIBERIUS. Is there injustice any longer in Rome, Mother?

CORNELIA: When you are a man, you will judge for yourself, Tiberius.

GAIUS: Now tell us the story of Horatius and how he held the wooden bridge!

CORNELIA: Not now, Gaius, for it is time that you were both in bed. A noble matron comes to visit me this evening, and how can I be troubled with two noisy boys? Be off with you, and I shall bid Servius attend you.

(*Exeunt Tiberius and Gaius. R.*)

(*Cornelia claps her hands. Enter Servius, a slave. L.*)

Prepare the bath for the boys, Servius, and see that Gaius washes behind his ears. (*Exit Servius, R.*)

(*Enter woman slave, L.*)

SLAVE: The lady Julia, Madam. . . .

(*Enter Julia, a rich and well-dressed matron. Exit slave*)

JULIA: My dear Cornelia!

CORNELIA: Pray be seated.

JULIA: My dear Cornelia—I hope you will forgive me—but there is something which I *must* say to you, even if you should be **angry** with me.

CORNELIA: And what is that?

JULIA: You are the daughter of Scipio, a matron of one of the noblest families in Rome—and yet you refuse to marry again—you who could choose among the greatest. Even princes have sought your hand, and now—is it not so, for it is spoken of everywhere—

Ptolemy of Egypt has laid his crown at your feet: Cornelia, you could be a *Queen*!

CORNELIA (*smiling*): And what has a Roman to do with crowns and thrones? Did we not banish them with Tarquin?

JULIA: But to be Queen of Egypt! O Cornelia, I pray you, do not refuse! I should still be your friend, you know. I should visit you.

CORNELIA: I think it better for Rome that I devote myself to the education of my two boys. Since their father died, as you know, that has been my chief task ... I am sorry to disappoint you, Julia, but I wish my boys to grow up as Romans, not Egyptians!

JULIA: And to think of the jewels you could wear! See this necklace which my husband brought me from Africa! Is it not beautiful? ... These rings also ...

CORNELIA: They are indeed beautiful, Julia.

JULIA: And this jewelled comb. ...

CORNELIA: These are lovely things.

JULIA: And now—do show me some of *your* treasures, Cornelia.

CORNELIA (*rising and moving towards exit, R.*): Gladly.

JULIA (*looking off*): Your two little boys!

CORNELIA: *These* are my jewels, O Julia; the only ones of which I am proud.

CURTAIN

SCENE II

The same. Some years later.
Cornelia is seated, sewing. Enter Tiberius.

TIBERIUS: Mother!

CORNELIA (*rising*): My son! back home from Spain!
What have the long years grown in thee,
What fruits have ripened? Taller thou art,
And seeming wiser—is it so?

TIBERIUS: Not yet so wise but that I need
    Thy wisdom, Mother. Nights and days
    Through weary months I've pondered deep,
    And now my head is charged with thoughts,
    My heart with burning visions . . . Rome
    Is full of ills . . . The state is sick . . .
    As through the countryside we marched—
    There in the fields were gangs of slaves,
    Chained, for the rich have all the land.
    And when the soldier from his wars
    Limps homeward, what reward has he?
    What portion of that precious earth
    For which he gave his blood? I say,
    New laws must rise in Rome, new thoughts,
    New deeds—that Romans may enjoy
    The crumbs of Justice. Now I go
    To stand before the people, there
    To offer them myself as Tribune.
    So may I hope to make new laws.
    Have I thy blessing, Mother?

CORNELIA: Yea, to be sure. May all the gods
    Prosper thy way . . . I have been called
    Cornelia, daughter of Scipio.
    But men shall in the days to come
    Name me anew—Cornelia,
    Mother of the Gracchi . . .

              (*Enter Octavius*)

TIBERIUS: Welcome, Octavius, my friend!
    Now is the hour when thou and I
    March forward. We shall be
    Two Tribunes, if the people will—
    And they shall will it, when they hear
    The flaming truth our tongues shall tell.

OCTAVIUS: Beware the Patricians! They have caught
    Some breath of this, foresee their land
    Parcelled among Plebeians, cry:
    This is the end, the end of Rome!

TIBERIUS: 'Tis not the end, but a beginning.
They must obey the people's voice.
If but the Tribunes all agree,
There's naught to fear. The people now
Are crowding into Rome—let's hence
And speak to them . . .

(*Exit Tiberius and Octavius*)

CURTAIN

SCENE III

The Forum

Crowd. Senator speaking from the rostrum.

SENATOR: This Tribune ye have chosen, he
Tiberius Gracchus, will pretend
That all your ills shall now be healed
With just a little land. But who,
I ask, shall till your land?
How shall the soldier, called to war,
Having no slaves, return to find
His acres ploughed, his harvest done?
And how, with land unploughed, unsown,
Shall ye find food to eat? Beware
Of witless talk, and trust in those,
Your Senators, whose wisdom lies
In quiet thought and length of years.

(*Exit*)

TIBERIUS (*leaping up*): The landowners have lied to you
With tales of hunger, want and woe.
Their stars are setting, and they fear
Lest at the clamour of your voice
They lose the land your fathers bought
With blood of battle. 'Tis their aim

To keep all for themselves and sell
  Their slave-reaped corn to you ...
  Is it not mockery to exhort
  Soldiers to fight for household gods,
  For altars which they never had,
  Ancestral graves they never owned?
  To call them—'ere the battle's joined—
  "Lords of the earth", who have no clod
  On which to set one foot and say:
  "This piece of land is mine?"
  Hearken, O Romans, there's a law,
  An ancient law long since forgot,
  Which says "No citizen shall own
  More than so much of Roman earth".
  This was the old Licinian Law,
  It needs but now your general voice.
  Declare: "This law shall be restored,"
  And every citizen shall plough
  The land his fathers bought for Rome.

OCTAVIUS (*stepping on the rostrum*):
  I am no enemy of the people,
  Nor would deny you corn or land,
  Yet, as a Tribune, I oppose
  This law, and utter "I forbid!"

     (*Descends*)

TIBERIUS (*following him*):
  Octavius! What means this deed?
  Why hast thou broken faith with me?

OCTAVIUS: Either I must break faith with thee,
  Or with my better judgment.

TIBERIUS: Who hath persuaded thee? What craft
  Has warped thy mind?

OCTAVIUS: None but my reason, which must be
  The light of every man.

TIBERIUS: Then is thy light grown dim. Perchance,
  Thine own broad acres made thee pause

And ponder on thy loss. If so,
I shall, from mine own purse, repay
An ample sum for every yard.

OCTAVIUS: Insult me not with vulgar bribes!
My mind is settled. I forbid!

TIBERIUS: That is a word I too may use!
I shall forbid, forbid, forbid
Every law and every act
And paralyse the State of Rome
Until this law is passed.

OCTAVIUS: Yet can'st thou not forbid my thoughts!

TIBERIUS: Not thoughts—but *thee* I may forbid!
For Thou, the Tribune who alone
Dost clog the stream of Justice, *thou*
May be forbidden by the State!
For surely whom the people choose
The people may cast out!

OCTAVIUS: Before a year has rolled its course
To do so were against the law!

TIBERIUS: What is the Law? The people's voice!
What say you, Romans? Shall this man—
Chosen by you to be your shield
Against Patrician tyranny—
Remain as Tribune, he who votes
Against your sacred rights?

CROWD: No, no, away with him (etc.)

TIBERIUS: Tomorrow then shall we decide
Before a full assembly. . . .

(Crowd drifts away)

OCTAVIUS (*calmly*): He who will not hear the law
Will one day cry to her himself
And find her deaf.

CURTAIN

SCENE IV

HOUSE OF CORNELIA
(Some years later)

(Cornelia, Gaius, Marcus and Lucia. Cornelia is seated. Gaius is restlessly moving about)

CORNELIA: Rest thee, Gaius, be at peace.
    Wisdom flows from quiet thought.

GAIUS: They have forsaken me, they look
    Coldly upon me, pass me by,
    Give me no greeting in the street.
    Have they forgotten everything
    In two short months? Before I sailed
    For Carthage—there to build for them
    Another city, rich with land,
    I was their most-loved Tribune.
    Now—I'm but a stranger . . .

CORNELIA *(rising)*: Thine enemies worked cunningly,
    For, since they killed Tiberius,
    They have grown wiser, and they know
    Neglect is deadlier than to kill.
    Tiberius they killed, but yet
    They could not kill the laws he made.
    Death sanctified both him, and them.

MARCUS: But now *thy* laws they seek to change.

GAIUS: But how, and what and why, O Marcus?

MARCUS: Thy ship had scarcely left the quay
    When Drusus, their appointed voice,
    Began to fill the people's ears
    With windy promises. New land
    For colonies he'd find at home
    In Italy—not far away
    In distant Africa—and here
    Would be no taxes!

GAIUS: But such land
   Is nowhere to be found!

LUCIA: That is no matter. 'Tis enough
   That Drusus said it, and the Plebs
   Believed him, while forgetting thee.

MARCUS: That is their plan. And with thy scheme
   Made seeming foolish, and thyself
   Forgotten, 'tis an easy step
   To have the law repealed, Carthage
   Left barren, and renew the cry:
   "The ground is cursed where Carthage stood."

GAIUS: Outrageous! How they lie and lie,
   Deceive the simple folk, and take
   All to themselves! What ails this Senate?

MARCUS: They are afraid of thee. They say
   "This Gracchus is more dangerous
   Than e'er his brother was."

GAIUS: I see.
   Then shall I prove it. If they try
   To change the law, I shall make known
   The truth to all the people, show
   How grossly they have been deceived,
   And so regain their favour.

MARCUS: Then act with speed, for but today
   I hear that orders have gone out
   Summoning the tribes to vote.
   They lose no time, these Senators,
   Knowing thou hast returned to Rome.

GAIUS: Quick, Marcus, bid what friends are left
   To gather on the Capitol.
   There shall we pass a watchful night
   Ready to meet what fateful day
   May bring us.

   MARCUS: Shall they come with arms?

GAIUS: I care not. I shall go unarmed.
    My weapons are my voice and tongue.

MARCUS: Arms would be wiser. We shall meet
    Within the hour. I'll summon them.
    Let Fulvius be in command.

(Exit)

LUCIA: Gaius, my husband, wilt thou go
    To give thy body to the swords
    Of those who slew Tiberius?
    Is it not fruitless? They have power.
    Thou can'st not stem the river's flood;
    And, like a helpless, fallen leaf,
    They'll sweep thee to the sea. Have pity!
    Thou hast children—and a wife . . .

(Gaius draws himself gently from her and goes out)

(She sinks to the ground, weeping)

(Cornelia bends over her as the curtain falls)

SCENE V

THE CAPITOL HILL

Opimius and Fabius, the Consuls, with Senators and Soldiers.

FABIUS: The Gracchan mob has now encamped
    Upon the Aventine. Last night
    They slew my servant as he brought
    The offering from the temple. Thus
    Doth noble Gracchus treat the poor!

OPIMIUS: It is an act of civil war
    To seize and hold by force of arms
    A place within the city. Go,
    Declare it to the citizens
    That these are enemies of Rome.

(Exit Soldier)

(*Enter young Fulvius*)

Whom have we here? Who art thou, boy?

YOUNG FULVIUS: I come from Fulvius, O Consul,
To bring thee from the friends of Gracchus
Words of peace. They have no wish
To run to arms, nor yet to raise
One sword 'gainst any man of Rome.
Thus would they gladly speak with thee.

FABIUS: Then wherefore did they kill my slave
Upon this very hill?

YOUNG FULVIUS: Of that, O Consul, I know naught,
Saving that Gracchus wept with wrath
That such a deed was done.

OPIMIUS: Go, say to Fulvius and Gracchus:
The Consuls make no terms with rebels.
First, let their followers disperse,
Then shall they come before the Senate
To answer for their deeds. And now,
We march upon the Aventine.
Make haste—if they would answer.

(*Exit young Fulvius*)

What man shall bring to me the head
Of this rebellious Gracchus,
Shall have its weight in gold.

(*Dim out and Exeunt*)

(*Noise of shouting, off*)

(*Enter Gaius, Servius and three friends*)

1ST FRIEND: 'Most all have fled, save but a few
Who'll be your rearguard—Run!
We'll join them. Here they come,
Fighting like tigers. Run, I say!
Stay not! Valour's a wasted life!

(*Exeunt Gaius and Servius, L. Enter soldiers, R. driving back friends of Gracchus. They are joined by three others and all are driven off, L.*)
(*Shouting continues*)
(*After a pause, Enter Gaius and Servius, L. back*)

GAIUS: There's no escape, yet here we have
A moment's pause for breath. Servius!
Thou art my slave, at my command.
One last command I give thee, then
Thou shalt be free. Thou hast a dagger.
Slay me, ere I'm ta'en alive.

SERVIUS (*strikes Gaius dead*): Now, Master, I will follow thee.

(*He stabs himself and falls across his master's body*)

(*Noise of shouting draws nearer. Slow curtain*)

SCENE VI

HOUSE OF CORNELIA

(*Cornelia is standing. Marcus has just entered*)

CORNELIA: Thou bringest news.

MARCUS: Gaius is dead,
By his own hand, or by his slave's,
Who, by the self-same dagger, lay
Dead across his master. There,
In a grove the soldiers found him . . .
There was no time for him to flee . . .
They offered peace if we'd disband,
But reckless Fulvius refused,
And when the troops advanced on us
He was the first to flee. He too
Is dead. Some, like Horatius,
Did hold the bridge for Gaius' sake,
But all too soon the tide swept on.
There was a price upon his head,

> The weight of that same head in gold . . .
> The river Tiber has the rest.
> Weep not, dear lady, for he died
> As e'er the noblest Roman did
> On field of battle.

CORNELIA: O it were precious gold indeed,
> Which could outweigh that head. Thou Tiber,
> Nourisher of Rome, thou stream
> Of life-blood, into thee are poured
> The lives of my two sons. So may
> This noble sap make rich the days
> Of generations yet to come.
> To thy deep flood I'll add no tears.
> I am to proud to weep.

SLOW CURTAIN

THE DEATH OF JULIUS CAESAR

(age 11-12)

This again is a play more suited to the older children of the age-group. Broadly speaking, it follows Shakespeare's story up to the point of Mark Antony's speech at Caesar's funeral. The actual Shakespeare is of course too difficult for children of this age, not only as regards the language but the five-foot line is too "heavy" for them to handle. They need a less subtle rhythm. The author freely admits that he wrote this play with continual trepidation, the constant problem being to avoid producing a mere simplified rehash of Shakespeare, which would have been monstrous. On this account he has kept away from the details of "Julius Caesar" as much as possible, but where he has been obliged to come nearer to certain vital passages he has tried to make every line his own and in only one case has he made use of one that is not, namely in Mark Antony's funeral speech—"These are honourable men". This was necessary in order to bring out the satire and subtle persuasiveness of the oration. He apologises to anyone who may think the whole attempt presumptuous, but it seemed the only way of enabling children of this age to act this story.

SCENE I

A ROOM IN BRUTUS' HOUSE

CASCA: Rome knows herself no more, my friends,
    She shrouds her heart, no longer wears
    The garment of nobility.
    When Cincinnatus left his plough
    To smite with clean toil-hardened hands
    The ancient foes of Rome, no thought
    Had he of vain ambition,—no—
    Nor wished for any recompense—
    But only to return in peace
    Unto his field again . . .
    There was a Rome indeed—but now
    Their *hearts* are hard, and grasping hands
    Tremble to reach at kingly power.

CASSIUS: It is not only nobleness
    And simple ways, that lie forgot—
    But Rome did once respect her laws.
    These sat enthroned, no ruler dared
    To count himself above the law,
    Lest by one deed he might defame
    Its sacred power; and there were those
    Who sent their very sons to death
    Rather than wound one law. But where,
    O Brutus, are such Romans now?
    They tramp, instead, the laws to death
    Beneath the feet of arméd men,
    And he is master of the law
    Who masters legions. Thus enthroned
    Sits Caesar, master of us all.

BRUTUS: But we ourselves did seat him there,
    Dictator for his span of life,
    And so the chains that bind our wrists
    We did ourselves put on. Besides,
    Was not this Caesar merciful?
    Did he not spare the lives of us
    Who fought at Pompey's side? . . .
    He is my friend, and ye must show
    Some weightier reason, ere I raise
    My sword to strike him down.

DECIMUS: What charioteer who, giving rein
    To some high-mettled horse, and sees
    The wrecking of his chariot
    Unless he curb his flight—would say:
    "I may not interfere with him,
    "I may not take the freedom back
    "That first I gave"—and lets the horse
    Pull driver, chariot, to their doom?
    Shall we, who gave this Caesar power,
    Not lay our hands upon the rein
    And stay his headlong course?

BRUTUS: What headlong course? To what abyss

Doth Caesar drag our empire down?
In all our borders there is peace
And Rome is mistress of the world.

TREBONIUS: Peace there may be,—but freedom—where?
So also is there peace in prison!
All that our forefathers have built
Since kings became a banished race—
This, Caesar soon will bring to nought.
The Senate's power, the people's voice,
The consul's dignity and sway—
Where are they even now? What then
May not this tyrant do? . . .
I say, there will be kings in Rome
And Tarquin's day will come again,
If we withhold our laggard hands
And let this Caesar live.

BRUTUS: Then must he die. For all must die
Who murder freedom—is't not so?
Or do we in this killing, kill
The very liberty we love?
If we do slay a tyrant—say—
Are we, too, not tyrannical?
O Fates, between whose awful hands
Our deeds are moulded and the shape
Of future days and years begotten—
May we not glimpse the teeming dark,
Have vision of what things may come
Out of the deeds we do? . . . My friends,
If I do join with you in this—
If I must slay the man I love,
Remember that, whate'er I do,
Is done for Rome alone. Farewell.

(*Exeunt all but Brutus,* CURTAIN)

SCENE II

Caesar's House

(Early morning)
(Sound of bell)

(Enter Steward: clapping his hands, and shouting to slaves, as they enter)

STEWARD: Come up! ye sluggards! 'Tis the dawn.
Make clean our master's audience-room!
Polish each pillar and make shine
The many-coloured patterned floor.
Yon spider and his dusty web
Chase from his home, and let me see
No dust upon the cornice-edge.
You others, clean the banquet-hall
Of yester-evening's supper. Ho!
Come up, ye sluggards! 'Tis the dawn!

(Exit Steward)

1ST SLAVE: A sumptuous supper Caesar gave.

2ND SLAVE: Wert there?

1ST SLAVE: Aye. Lobster garnished with asparagus, mullets, lampreys, goose's liver, roast calf, roast boar, mushrooms and apples—with wine from Spain, Gaul, and Africa, all cooled with snow.

3RD SLAVE: Any titbits?

1ST SLAVE: Nay. The guests took them all away in their napkins.

4TH SLAVE: Was Caesar merry?

5TH SLAVE: He ate but little and seemed thoughtful. I listened to the talk as the wine went round,—strange talk, it was, for so fair a supper. They spoke of death.

6TH SLAVE: Of *death*?

5TH SLAVE: They spoke of what manner of death they would choose to die. Caesar took little part in their talk, for he was busy with letters I had brought to him. He looked up once and said: "I should choose a sudden one", and continued with his reading.

6TH SLAVE: Ah, 'tis little likely he should die a hasty death—so well-beloved and guarded as he is.

7TH SLAVE: I would not be an emperor.
Give me the thund'ring chariot,
Four pounding stallions in my grasp,
The roaring circus, and the race
Wheel against wheel, in sun and dust.
Then is he king—the charioteer—
Though he be slave or hireling. Now
All eyes, all hearts are fixed on him
And even emperors are swayed
By his deft moving hands . . .

4TH SLAVE: Wouldst be a chariot-driver, Fulvius?

7TH SLAVE: Aye, would I were! Then would ye see
A race beyond all races. Here,
In the chariot stall I stand and wait,
Helmet on head and whip in hand,
My reins about my body. Now
The trumpet sounds, the rope falls down,
I move into the glittering line
And wait the signal. All is hushed.
My servants round me wish me well.
The trumpet sounds again. We're off!
My horses leap, I deftly gain
The inmost place, I hear the cries:
"Onward the Blue!" I reach the turn,

(*Other slaves cheer and wave encouragement*)

My left horse stumbles, but I urge
The outermost, and now we swing
Swiftly and safely round. The stretch
Lies clear before me. Like a flash
I reach the end and swing again.
"The Blue, the Blue, onward the Blue!"
They cry. But now, a rival wheel

   Runs close to mine, and at the bend
   We clash together, stagger, sway,
   I hear them cry "The Green is down!"
   And in the dust my rival sprawls. . . .

SLAVES: Hurrah! the Blue! Onward the Blue!

    (Enter Calpurnia with maid, Constantia)

CALPURNIA: What strange untimely noise is this?
   On with thy dusting, Fulvius!
   Lucius, seek thy master, say
   I would at once have speech with him.

    (Exeunt Slaves)

   Constantia—remain with me . . .
   Let no one come to speak with Caesar,
   Clients, or senators or friends.
   Admit no person to the house—
   Go—say to those who guard the door,
   Calpurnia commands them . . .

    (Exit Constantia)

    (Enter Caesar)

CAESAR: Thou bid'st me come, Calpurnia?

CALPURNIA: My Julius! the night has been
   Thick with foreboding. Shrieks and cries
   Unbodied, filled the troubled air,
   And flaming warriors were seen
   Embattled in the clouds. The heavens
   Were all alive with fitful fire,
   And Nature's dreadful auguries
   Were mirrored in my dreams. Go not,
   I pray thee, to the Senate House,
   But bide with me in peace until
   This evil day is past.

CAESAR: Why should these sights and sounds foretell
   An evil day for Caesar? Nay,
   Rather such mighty signs portend
   Some danger that is Rome's. If so,

'Tis not for me to skulk and hide,
But to be first where strikes the storm,
And therefore must I go.

CALPURNIA: If there be but one thunderbolt,
And that one aimed at Caesar?
Could Rome's misfortune be more great
Than some ill-chance to Caesar?
Julius, I beg thee, bear in mind
What late the soothsayer did say—
"Caesar, beware the Ides of March!"
And is not this the very time?

CAESAR: Why should I fear, and what should come
That Caesar has not many times
Opposed and conquered? Better to die
One death, than live in hourly fear.
The Senate awaits me; I must go.

CALPURNIA: Though Caesar fears not, I do fear.
Call *me* the coward, let my will
Rule thee but once, for these few hours,
Or else my fear. Let word be sent
That thou art sick and cannot come.

CAESAR: So Caesar plays the coward's trick,
And lies.

CALPURNIA: The lie, too, shall be mine.
And all the shame, if thou wilt give
These hours to me that now the Fates
Do offer to my hands.

(She kneels)

CAESAR: Then take their gift, and send thou word . . .

(Exit Calpurnia)

(Enter Slave)

SLAVE: Most noble Caesar, there are some
Who seek thee, and who stand without.

CAESAR: Then bid them enter. What should stay
   Their present coming?

SLAVE: Caesar, those
   Who guard the door and have command
   That none this day should enter.

CAESAR: Whose command?

SLAVE: Calpurnia's.

   (Enter Calpurnia)

CAESAR: Not only may I not go hence,
   My very door is to be shut
   Against my friends! Let them come in!

   (Exit Slave)

CALPURNIA: O Caesar, this command I gave
   'Ere I could speak with thee. Beware,
   Lest now they tempt thee to go forth,
   Against thy promise. I have sent
   Our message to Mark Antony.

   (Enter Decimus)

DECIMUS: Good morrow, Caesar. I am come
   To bear you company. Your slaves
   At first did bar me. Is it so,
   That you are ill, as they did say?

CAESAR: I said not so. But I do say
   I cannot—will not—come with you.

DECIMUS: You are not ill, yet cannot come?

CAESAR: Will not. But tomorrow, yes.

DECIMUS: This is most strange. What shall I say
   To the awaiting Senators?

CALPURNIA: You have no need, for I have sent
   A message to Mark Antony,
   And he shall speak for Caesar—

CAESAR: Saying
    That I am ill, Calpurnia?

DECIMUS: Mark Antony has joined with those
    Who stand without, and Brutus too.
    He has received no message.

CAESAR: Say simply that I will not come.
    Simplest is best, and 'tis the truth.
    But for your own and private ear,
    'Tis rather that my wife is sick,
    With dreams and strange forebodings. These,
    She fears, spell danger to myself
    Should I go forth today.

DECIMUS: What dreams, good lady, trouble you?

CALPURNIA: Three times I dreamt that in my arms
    I held a corpse with many wounds,—
    And it was Caesar that I held.
    Then from his marble statue flowed
    His life-blood in a hundred streams,
    While many Romans joyously
    Did bathe their hands therein.

DECIMUS: Dear lady, this is not a dream
    Of dread import, but clearly shows
    How noble Caesar bleeds for us,
    How with such pity he is torn
    For those he rules, and how we all
    Are nourished by his sacrifice.
    It is a dream most fortunate,
    And one to give you joy . . .
    O Caesar, must it hence be said
    That Caesar could not stir abroad
    Until his wife had dreamed a dream
    More pleasing to her mind?

CAESAR: Thou see'st, Calpurnia, how a dream
    Of horrid semblance may conceal
    Fair purport and be innocent.

Decimus, thou hast read it well—
Should aught withhold me now?

(Enter Brutus, Mark Antony and others)

CAESAR: And see
What goodly company is here—
Brutus, Mark Antony, Cassius, all,
Most welcome, friends. I beg you grant
Forgiveness for this rude delay!
My robe, Calpurnia. See what friends
I have as escort. What defence
Could Caesar wish for more? Lead on!
'Twill be a joyous journeying.

(Exeunt all but Calpurnia)

CURTAIN

SCENE III

A Street

(Crowd awaiting Caesar)

1ST CITIZEN: Which way should Caesar come?

2ND CITIZEN: This way.
I have a suit to proffer him.

3RD CITIZEN: And I. Think you he reads himself
What we do write—or but his servants?

ARTEMIDORUS: For Caesar's sake alone, I pray,
That he will look on mine.

4TH CITIZEN: What is your plea?

ARTEMIDORUS: I must not tell,
It is a suit that touches him,
And life and death are poised in it.

4TH CITIZEN: Ha! Soothsayer, show your mystic art!
Say what is written in his scroll!

SOOTHSAYER: My vision reaches not so far.—
  But I do also fear this day.

1ST CITIZEN: See—now he comes—with Brutus, Cassius,
  Antony, and many more. . . .

  (*Enter Caesar and Senators*)

2ND CITIZEN: I beg you, noble Caesar, read!

3RD CITIZEN: A plea, O Caesar, hear my suit!

CAESAR (*to Soothsayer*): Well, friend, the Ides of March are come.

SOOTHSAYER: Aye, but not gone, O Caesar.

ARTEMIDORUS: Great Caesar, read this scroll, I pray,
  Ere you go further.

DECIMUS: Trebonius begs you that you read
  This suit that doth concern him closely.

ARTEMIDORUS: Nay, Caesar, do you read mine first,
  For 'tis a suit concerning Caesar!

DECIMUS: Fellow, how dare you block our path!

  (*Thrusts him aside*)

ARTEMIDORUS: Caesar, delay no more, but read!

CASSIUS: And is it thus you speak to Caesar?

CASCA: If you have anything to urge
  Pray do so in the proper place,
  Not in the street!

  (*Exeunt all but Artemidorus and Soothsayer*)

ARTEMIDORUS:
  Caesar—I pray you—read!
  (*to Soothsayer*): Alas—he knows not of his fate
  And will not know, unless he read.

SOOTHSAYER: The Ides of March have come. The stars
  Have spoken.

CURTAIN

SCENE IV

THE SENATE HOUSE

(Enter Caesar and Senators)

CASSIUS *(in low tone)*: Trebonius, remember now
 To draw Mark Antony apart
 And hold him deep in converse.

TREBONIUS: Mark Antony—a word with you—

(Exeunt Trebonius and Antony)

DECIMUS *(to conspirators)*: Let now Metellus Cimber speak.
 No time's to lose—or else we fail.

BRUTUS: See, he comes near; draw closely round.

CINNA: Casca—you are the first to strike.
 Watch for Metellus Cimber's signal.

CAESAR: Are all attentive to proceed
 With this day's business? What new pleas
 Have we in hand?

METELLUS: Most mighty Caesar, I do bring
 A suit that's nearest to my heart—
 My banished brother, Publius,—
 That he be pardoned—and return.

CAESAR: How oft, Metellus, have you asked
 This private favour? But your heart
 O'erlooks the public reason. Go,
 And find me argument enough
 Why now I should reverse decrees
 I made in sober judgment. Then,
 Perchance we may consider it.
 I punish not from passion's haste,
 So neither will I alter it
 For sake of passion's pleading.

BRUTUS: May not my own entreaty, Caesar,
 Weigh heavier than reason?

CAESAR: Why Brutus? Is this too thy suit?

CASSIUS: O Caesar, let me add my plea. (*Kneeling*)

CINNA: And I, too, Caesar, beg of you. (*Kneeling*)

CAESAR: Why bow to me? Am I a fool
To flatter with your crooked knees?—
Some petty king, whose waxen will
Bends to a favoured voice? Stand up,
Dishonour not this Senate-House
With fond un-Roman fawning!
Metellus has my answer. 'Tis enough.

BRUTUS: Is this then all?

CAESAR: My final word.

(*Metellus pulls Caesar's robe*)

CASCA: Thou speakest truth. I'll make it so!

(*Stabs him*)

CAESAR: Vile Casca! What is this? (*Others stab him*)
So many daggers!
Brutus,—even thou! (*Falls dead*)

BRUTUS: 'Tis done ... Good people, Senators,
Be not afraid; stand still, and hear!

(*Exeunt others*)

(*Enter Trebonius*)

DECIMUS: Here's one good friend—Trebonius.
What news of Antony?

TREBONIUS: He's fled,
As others when they saw the deed,
And rumour, like a roaring flame,
Makes spreading pathways through the town.
Men stand amazed, or wildly run,
And half-believe and half-deny.
'Tis urgent that we publish forth
Our reasons for the deed.

CASSIUS: Come, let us to the street, and cry:
"Freedom is come to Rome again!"

CASCA: And with our weapons still unwashed
Show them that tyranny is dead.

DECIMUS: Come all—and Brutus lead the way!

(Enter Mark Antony)

ANTONY: Stay! ere you leave this deed behind,
Permit Mark Antony to speak.
I know not what your purpose is,
Nor whose the blood must next be spilled;
But I would hear now from your mouths
If I am in your catalogue.
If so, as I was Caesar's friend,
This were the place most fit to die,
And I, by these same reeking swords,
Most honoured. But, if it be so
That I am counted as your friend,
And that you are prepared to show
How Caesar merited his death,
Then I may take you by the hands
And utter no discourtesy.

BRUTUS: Mark Antony, no swords of ours
Are turned towards you, nor indeed
Sought we the death of any man
Save Caesar. That you were his friend
Makes you no less a part of us,
For I who joined to strike him down
Did greatly love him.

ANTONY: I thank you and am satisfied,
If you will grant me this request,
That I may speak, in reverence due,
Of Caesar at his funeral.

BRUTUS: 'Tis granted, if you speak alone
Of what is due in Caesar's praise,
While I shall show the purposes
That lay behind our deed.

THE DEATH OF JULIUS CAESAR

ANTONY: I am agreed and thus in token
    Take you by the hands. (*Shakes hands with each*)

BRUTUS: Caesar's body now I give
    Into your care, that you may make
    All rightful preparation. Friends,
    The time awaits us—let us go.

(*Exeunt all but Antony*) (*Their voices are heard, shouting:* "*Freedom is come to Rome.*" "*Tyranny is dead.*" "*Caesar is no more.*" "*Rejoice, O citizens, for Liberty is here*")

(*As the sounds die away, Antony approaches Caesar's body*)

ANTONY: O Caesar, if thy soul can know
    The tumult of men's hearts, thou'lt hear
    The mounting storm in mine. No tongue,
    No tears, no cry of lamentation,
    Can loose this flood, nor give a name
    To this most devilish destruction.
    Here in this shattered temple lay
    The choicest spirit of our age,
    Now driven from his dwelling-place
    By th'envious knives of little men.
    So mute, so pitiful thou art,
    As pleading to the gods on high
    And dumbly crying out to men
    For justice. Let me take thy hand—
    Not as I did those murderers'—
    But swearing now a sacred oath:
    "I will not rest until this Rome
    Is purged of Caesar's enemies,
    And all my craft of tongue and hand
    Is bent into so fierce a spring,
    That were I alone against the world
    My will shall shape this end." Farewell,
    Thy book is closed; and now to write
    Upon the still unblotted page
    Another tale. . . .

CURTAIN

SCENE V

The Forum

(Crowd of citizens, listening to Brutus' speech, Mark Antony standing by. The body of Caesar lies on a bier)

CROWD: Long live Brutus! Noble Brutus, to rid us of this Caesar! He was a tyrant. Brutus and Cassius did right! Down with all tyrants! Let Rome be free! We want no kings in Rome! Long live Brutus!

BRUTUS: Now have I shown to you my friends
That, striking down the man I loved,
There was no malice in my dagger,
But love for Rome; and were that love
Not greater than for Caesar,—then
Most justly should you censure me.
Caesar was honourable and brave,
But fierce ambition is a canker
That kills the worth it feeds on. So
We slew him, ere the illness grew
To fatten on the health of Rome.
Thus shall ye do for Brutus too
When'er I so infect the State.

CROWD: Noble Brutus! 'Twas rightly done. Long live Brutus!

BRUTUS: In praise of Caesar's better parts
Here is Mark Antony to speak,
As due in Caesar's funeral.

CROWD: We will not hear him! Away with Antony!
He was a friend of Caesar. Down with tyranny!
Let's follow Brutus!

BRUTUS: Peace, friends! I wish no followers.
Allow me to depart alone.
Do you remain in quietness
And hearken now to Antony.
He has our leave to speak to you.
I pray you hear him patiently.

(Exit)

THE DEATH OF JULIUS CAESAR

CROWD: Let us hear Antony. Aye, if he be just to Brutus.
  Peace! Let him speak!

ANTONY: My friends, my countrymen, I come
  With simple words and good intent,
  Neither to praise nor to condemn,
  To speak of Caesar what is due
  To all great men who die.
  For was he not the conqueror
  Of many lands, which brought to Rome
  A glory she had never known
  And ransoms like a stream of gold?
  Thus was he father to us all,
  But yet ambitious, Brutus says,—
  A strange ambition, was it not,
  To do so much for Rome?
  But these are honourable men
  And have good cause for what they do.

CROWD: Aye, 'twas strange! This Caesar did bring great
  wealth to the city! And honour too!

ANTONY: Perchance it was that to be king
  Was Caesar's dark ambition, yet
  You know that I did offer thrice
  To crown him with a crown of gold,
  And thrice he did refuse.
  A strange ambition, was it not?
  To cast aside a crown?
  Yet Brutus and his friends agree
  He was ambitious, and we know
  That they are honourable men.

CROWD: Perchance this Caesar was not ambitious! He cast the crown
  aside! Surely he has been wronged! Hearken again to Antony!

ANTONY: Here lies the ruined citadel
  That once was Caesar. In these walls
  There lived a noble soul, with heart
  To pity, and with hands to heal.
  Once all men loved him, and no tongue

Had learned these idle whisperings;
But now have Brutus and his friends
Spoken with tongues of steel, and stilled
That tongue which could have answered them.
I know not what that tongue might say,
But honourable men have said
He was ambitious, and no doubt
'Tis best to slay ambitious men.

CROWD: Honourable men! 'Tis true we did love Caesar!
Caesar has been wronged! These men are traitors!
Murderers! Caesar must be avenged!

ANTONY: My friends, these words are mutinous!
I must not move you to such thoughts,
For they do wrong these honest men
Who murdered Caesar. I may but tell
What I do know—how Caesar loved you.
Here is his will, wherein he leaves
To every citizen of Rome
Seventy-five drachmas—thus you see
Caesar had made you all his heirs!

CROWD: O noble Caesar! We will avenge him! Death to the traitors!
Death to Brutus!

ANTONY: Be patient, for 'tis not the end.
The will speaks of his parks and orchards
Beside the Tiber. These he leaves
To you, O citizens, for ever!
Was ever Caesar such as this?

CROWD: Never! Never! Come, let us fire the houses of these traitors!
Take benches, tables, doors, anything! Revenge! Kill! Fire!
Slay! Let every traitor die!

(Exeunt Citizens)

ANTONY: Fire and ruin, death, revenge,
Sweep your monstrous wings above us!
So may thy spirit rest, O Caesar!

CURTAIN

ST. COLUMBA

(age 12–13)

This represents simply three short scenes taken from the "Life of St. Columba" by St. Adamnan who became Abbot of Iona in A.D. 679 to which island Columba had come in 563. The scenes deal with Columba's arrival, his treatment of a robber, and the day of his death. The scenes are written in rhyming verse, this appearing to the writer as being more appropriate to the subject.

SCENE I

A HILLTOP ON IONA
(May 12th, A.D. 563)

(Enter Columba, climbing)

COLUMBA: The dim blue hills have died away
    Behind the western sea, and grey
    The ocean stretches endlessly.
    Here may we fold our wings at last,
    Here shelter from the stormy blast.
    Here shall we labour, here fulfil
    Our earthly task, our Master's will.
    O, but how gaily my coracle danced
    On the sea, on the sea where the white wings glanced,
    The while my sad heart was bleeding, and yet
    My cheeks with the spray and the tears were wet,
    And my face towards Derry. O then I bewailed
    The errand that brought me, the mountains that paled
    And melted like clouds in the heaven above,
    As I looked back on Erin, the land that I love.
    But weak is the man who fears to lead.
    Who dares not look upon the deed
    That waits the doing.   Diormit, my friend.

(Enter Diormit)

Here stand we at our journey's end.
See how the waters meet the skies . . .
No trace to tell where Erin lies,
Nor tempt the tender heart to stray
Out of the hard and holy way.

DIORMIT: This isle is blesséd. See how bright
The flowers glow, the heavenly light
That slumbers in the stones beside
The sea so green and purple dyed.

COLUMBA: Here dwells a peace which stirs the heart . . .
Diormit, we have no longer part
In yon green land, its many lives,
Nor shall we see its men, its wives,
Ever again. Those faded flowers
We call the past are ever ours—
And drop their seeds to bud anew
Around our feet in season due.
So grieve not. Let the earth close o'er
Whatever's past, and on this shore
Of longing let us bury deep
The ship that brought us, and so keep
Our hearts' high courage. Haste away!
Ho, there! Bury the boat, I say!

CURTAIN

SCENE II

"The Robber"

(*Enter Columba and Diormit*)

COLUMBA (*sitting*): Let us tarry here awhile.
Yonder, on the Mulean Isle
Lies a robber who would steal
Our sea-calves from the Isle of Seal.
Last night from Colonsay he came—

Ere Mocudruidi his name—
And now lies hid from light of day
Beneath his boat. His wrongful prey
In darkness he would seize, and run
Homeward with the early sun.
But we shall speak with him anon.
Two of the brethren have gone
To seek him—and fulfilled their quest!
Here comes our most unwilling guest.

(Enter Silnan with Robber)

SILNAN: Beneath his boat I saw him lie,
Surely as thou didst prophesy!

ROBBER: Holy father, here I swear
My innocence. I would not dare
To slay thy seals, or aught of thine.
I am a fisherman. My line
I cast by night, and sleep by day,
And surely fish are lawful prey!

COLUMBA: Nor hook nor line has thou, but near
Thine upturned boat a ready spear
Lies buried in the shallow sand.
Oft hast thou broken God's command
"Thou shalt not steal." Thy thievish heart
Hath played too long its greedy part.
If thou art hungry or in need
Come thou to us, and we with speed
Shall freely give what thou dost ask,
And get thee to some lawful task!
Silnan, go quickly, kill some sheep
To give our brother, that he keep
His soul from sin, nor turn his face
Empty to his dwelling-place.

(Exit Diormit and Silnan)

(Robber kneels before Columba)

CURTAIN

SCENE III

The Last Journey
(June 9th, A.D. 597)

(Diormit, seated, writing. Enter Silnan)

SILNAN: Diormit, tell me now, I pray,
   The doings of this holy day,
   For far afishing have I been
   And nothing have I heard or seen,
   But yet, as by the beat of wings,
   My heart is stirred by nameless things.

DIORMIT: Our aged father, weak and worn,
   Was early in the wagon borne
   To see the tillers of the soil
   And there to bless them at their toil.
   Then gently did he speak, and say:
   "Long have I wished to pass away
   To Christ the Lord: and this request
   He now doth grant me, and a rest
   From all my labour." Thus he spake,
   And we were dumb for sadness' sake,
   And when unloosened was our tongue,
   Our souls were mute as harps unstrung.

SILNAN: Alas! What shall befall this land
   Without our father's guiding hand?

DIORMIT: And when from sorrow we awoke
   He blessed this island and its folk
   And so returned the way he went.
   But yet was not his vigour spent,
   For to the granary he hied
   To bless the fruits of harvest-tide.
   Now came he home, and on the way
   He sat him on a stone to rest,
   When, lo, his horse with piteous neigh

Ran weeping to his master's breast,
And tears upon his lap he shed
The while our father stroked his head
And blessed him. And to me he saith:
"This poor dumb creature sorroweth,
For God hath to his heart revealed
That which from thine hath lain concealed,
O reasoning man!" And he arose
To watch the evening shadows close.

SILNAN: How sad a tale, and yet how blest!
I thank thee Diormit. I'll to rest.
There stirs strange music in my breast.

(Exit)

(Enter Columba)

COLUMBA: The book of psalms, Diormit. See
What's yet to do, and let us be
Busy with our task.

DIORMIT: But nay,
Good father, all this weary day
Thou hast known nothing of repose.
'Tis meet thou keep thy strength for those
Who need thee most—thy loving flock.

COLUMBA: I have a certain secret talk
To hold with thee, my trusted friend.
This night I come unto the end
Of all my days. The solemn hour
Of midnight from the belfrey tower
Shall ring to greet our Saviour's day.
And then to Him I take my way.

DIORMIT: Father, alas! Must it be so?

COLUMBA: Our Lord invites me, and I go.
These my last words I now commend
To all my flock. Do thou, my friend,
Faithfully their message tell:
"My sons, let love among you dwell,

Unfeigned and peaceful, so shall God
Bless the pathway ye have trod
And care for you in coming need,
While I abide and intercede
With Him in Heaven, that ye may see
The good things of Eternity."

DIORMIT: I shall do all that thou dost ask.

COLUMBA: Turn we to our unfinished task.
Write now these words:—
"O taste and see that the Lord is good; blessed is the man that trusteth in Him."
"O fear the Lord, ye His saints: for there is no want in them that fear Him."
"The young lions do lack and suffer hunger; but they that seek the Lord shall not want any good thing . . ."

(He pauses)

. . . They that seek, lack no good thing . . .

(Church bell begins to ring)

(Columba rises and runs towards door)

DIORMIT: My father, the midnight bell doth ring!

(Exit Columba)

Let me help thee on thy way!

(Exit Diormit)

(Off): Good brothers—to the church, I pray!
Haste ye with lights, bring lights, I say!

(Voices off): Bring lamps!
Bring lights!
O haste!
Who crieth?
Haste to the church!
Our father dieth!

(Enter Cormac)

CORMAC: Silnan, awake! Awake, I say!

(Enter Silnan)

Our father's soul doth pass away . . .
Before the altar steps he lieth . . .
Bring lights, bring lights, our father dieth!

(Exit)

SILNAN: *(stands looking: suddenly he has a vision of the soul of Columba after death)*:
Thou hast no need of light,
Thou pure and holy soul,
To guide thee in thy flight.
Behold the sea and sky
Ablaze with Angel's wings,
And thou, with hand on high,
Blessing our earthly things . . .
Thou hast no need of light.

CURTAIN

WIND ON THE WATERS

(age 12-13)

The next two plays are concerned with the Renaissance period, and this one deals with an incident in the life of Leonardo da Vinci. The event of the riot, round which the play is written, is an historical one. Some of the details, but not the characters of Leonardo's pupils depicted here, were suggested by Merejskowski's novel "The Forerunner". Opening on a quiet note the tension is gradually built up until the scene ends in a comical anti-climax. The play demands some good acting all round and should be attempted with only more mature children.

SCENE

Leonardo's Studio in Milan, About 1497

(Caesare—a pupil—at work on a painting, the back of which is towards audience.
Three repeated knocks at the door. Caesare is absorbed in his work and pays no attention.
At last, Enter Francesco, a boy of 13)

FRANCESCO: I pray you Sir, is this Master Leonardo's studio?

CAESARE: It is.

(Throughout the ensuing conversation he does not take his eyes from his work)

FRANCESCO: Are you . . . ?

CAESARE: No. The Master is out. What do you want with him? What is your name?

FRANCESCO: I hoped . . . I came to beg . . . that he might take me as his pupil. My name is Francesco.

CAESARE: The Master has many pupils—and mighty few ducats to keep us withal. Can you draw and paint?

FRANCESCO: I have brought a drawing to show to Master Leonardo.

CAESARE: Good. (*Continues painting*).

(*Pause*)

FRANCESCO: My father knows not of my coming hither. He wishes to apprentice me to Silvestro, the goldsmith. But *I* want to be a painter.

(*Pause*)

My father likes not Master Leonardo. He says he is a sorcerer and an infidel ... *Is* he a sorcerer, Sir?

CAESARE: Master Leonardo is a man of science, and chief engineer to the Duke. He studies mechanics—that is, the laws of movement,—and anatomy—that is, he cuts up the bodies of men and of animals to study and draw them. He builds canals, fortifications, engines of war,—and now he is making a machine with wings so that men may fly like birds.

FRANCESCO: Fly!

(*Enter Maturina, the housekeeper*)

MATURINA: Caesare, when does the master return? Think you he will bring supper with him? For in all the larder there is nought to eat. Did *anyone* ever see such a house as this? Full of machines, pictures, skeletons, instruments of alchemy, and a dozen of hungry folk—but neither food nor wine.

CAESARE: Perchance Marco brings something with him.

(*Enter Giovanni*)

GIOVANNI: I like this not, Caesare. There is trouble afoot.

CAESARE: Must I *never* have peace this day to finish my painting? Leave me, Giovanni!

GIOVANNI (*pacing about, and dancing round Caesare*): Listen, Caesare! You know that the Duke has given the sacred relic, the Holy Nail, to be placed in the Cathedral. Tomorrow is the solemn feast when it will be lodged in its golden casket high above the altar, and our master has designed a machine of ropes and pulleys wherewith it shall be raised to its place. He has been in the Cathedral until now with the Duke. Throughout the town there is much excitement, the citizens are thronging the streets, and there is some ugly talk. Many are enraged that the sacred relic has been entrusted to our master. "Leonardo, the infidel, the sorcerer, has been entrusted with the Holy Nail", they say, "Sacrilege! Down with Leonardo! Hang him! Burn him!" they cry. Has our Master returned?

MATURINA: Alas, no!

GIOVANNI: I greatly fear for him, Maturina. The mob will do him violence.

(*Enter Leonardo, with Marco, a pupil*)

LEONARDO (*off*): Aye, the contrivance worked well, Marco, and the Duke was much pleased.

GIOVANNI: God be praised! He is safe!... Did you pass safely through the rabble, Master?

LEONARDO: I saw no rabble. I came from the palace. Alas, my children, there is no peace in this world for a man to do his work. The good prior of the convent of Santa Maria delle Grazie is displeased with me. He complains to the Duke that I do not work industriously enough at my fresco of the Last Supper. There are days, he says, when I do nought but stand and stare at my work for hours on end. That is not like the gardeners in the good prior's garden who pick up their tools in the morning and lay them not down till the day is done—and so he told the Duke.

GIOVANNI: And what said you to the Duke, Master?

LEONARDO: I told him, Giovanni, that an artist works more intensely when he meditates than when he wields his brush—as his Excellence himself well knows.... The fresco is finished—but for two figures for whom I have not yet found a model. The one—I cannot hope to find on earth. The other—that of Judas—I fear will prove hard to find. "But," said I to the Duke, "if my search for a head of Judas should prove unavailing—I can always use that of the old prior"—at which his Excellence laughed heartily, and the prior was much discomfited.

(*All laugh*)

FRANCESCO *(approaching shyly)*: May it please your Worship—

LEONARDO: O-ho! Whom have we here?

CAESARE: A youth who would be your disciple, Master.

FRANCESCO *(kneeling and offering picture)*: Sir, would you deign to look at my poor work?

LEONARDO *(looks at picture and nods approvingly)*: See, Caesare,—here is promise, is there not? Now, my child, let me show you. . . .

MATURINA: Master Leonardo! Does your Worship wish for supper?

LEONARDO: Yes, yes,—supper, of course. We would all fain eat, I think. . . . See, my boy. . . .

MATURINA: But what shall we *eat*, Master?

LEONARDO: What you will, Maturina.

MATURINA: But Sir, there is nothing in the house.

LEONARDO: How is this, Marco? You are Warden. Why have you brought in no food?

MARCO: Food costs money, Master, and our treasury is empty.

LEONARDO: Empty? O, my children, where can our money have gone?

MATURINA: In machines, flying engines and other follies.

LEONARDO: Ah!—but we *have* money. I had all but forgotten. See—a gift from the Duke. A thousand ducats! Run, Maturina, buy us a rich repast: let us sup as we have never supped before! And our young friend here shall fare with us.

(Continues showing drawing to Francesco)

(Exit Maturina. Noise of rabble off, and a loud knocking)

MARCO: What noise is that?

(Enter Maturina)

MATURINA: Thieves! Robbers! Murderers! Holy Mother, have mercy upon us!

LEONARDO: What is amiss, Maturina?

MATURINA: There is a wild rabble at the door demanding entrance. They cry: Death to Leonardo! Death to the infidel!

GIOVANNI: I know. They demand the Nail, the Holy Nail.

LEONARDO: But I have it not. It is in the Cathedral in the Archbishop's keeping.

(*Uproar off*)

MATURINA (*wringing her hands*): What's to be *done*, Master?

LEONARDO: You have barred the door?

MARCO: I shall look from my window (*Exit*)

LEONARDO: Have we arms?

CAESARE: An old arquebus. I shall stand by the stair. (*Exit*)

(*Enter Marco*)

MARCO: 'Tis a crowd egged on by fanatical monks. They have sticks and torches. If the door yield not to their blows, I fear they will burn it.

(*Crash of glass. Maturina screams and runs off*)

LEONARDO (*to Francesco*): My boy, this is no fit place for you. How can we help him to escape, Giovanni?

FRANCESCO: Let *me* help, Master, I pray you!

LEONARDO: Help? How can *you* help, my son?

FRANCESCO: O Sir, if you will but let me down from a window, I shall summon the town guards. They pass at this hour.

LEONARDO: But the rabble will see you and kill you.

FRANCESCO: Nay, they know me not. They care not for me. Quick! a rope, good Master—or a blanket—

(*Exit, followed by Giovanni*)

LEONARDO: 'Tis a brave lad. God grant he will be saved.

MARCO: And what of us, Master? What shall we do?

LEONARDO: We have done all that we can, Marco. For the rest, let God's will be done.

(*Crash. Cries of "Infidel, infidel!"*)

(*Enter Giovanni*)

GIOVANNI: The lad is safe. Some spied him and gave chase, but others cried, "'Tis but a lad. 'Tis the sorcerer we want!" and he escaped into the darkness.

LEONARDO: God be praised! Tomorrow he will no longer wish to be my pupil. (*Noise*) Perhaps tomorrow there will be no master.

(*Crash. Enter Caesare*)

CAESARE: They have smashed the panel with an axe. Shall I fire?

LEONARDO: Nay, Caesare, let there be no bloodshed. Put that thing away. Stand back. 'Tis only me they seek.

(*Shouts: "Open, or we shall fire the house! Demon! Now we shall flay you! (Chanting) "Let God arise, let His enemies be scattered!" Ah! (Crash) One more stroke and the door is down!" (Crash) All listen, but there is silence*)

CAESARE: I hear a footstep on the stair.

LEONARDO: Stand back!

(*All wait, for a tense moment*)

(*Enter Francesco, pale and with head bleeding*)

FRANCESCO: They have gone, Master. The guard scattered them.

LEONARDO: But you bleed, my poor boy!

FRANCESCO: 'Tis but a stone one threw at me . . . I dared not go home . . . my father would be so angry. . . . (faints)

LEONARDO: Help me with him, Marco. (*They carry him to a couch*) Caesare, fetch Maturina! . . . Some water, Giovanni!

(*Exeunt Caesare and Giovanni*) (*Re-enter Giovanni with water and a towel*)

There, my brave boy—'twill soon heal. The wound is not deep.

And you shall sup with us after all—and be my pupil if you will. Lie still now.

(*Enter Caesare, who resumes painting*)

CAESARE: I have called Maturina.

LEONARDO: Where was Maturina?

CAESARE: In the cellar, hiding in a wine-cask ... An *empty* wine-cask.

(*Enter Maturina*)

MATURINA: Master Leonardo ...

LEONARDO: All is well, Maturina. The streets are safe again. At last you may go and buy our supper, and Marco will escort you.

MATURINA: But, Master Leonardo—a gentleman is here from the court, on an urgent matter!

(*Enter courtier*)

COURTIER (*bowing*): Master Leonardo, Her Excellence the Duchess bids you come *at once* to the palace. Will your Worship have the kindness to accompany me?

LEONARDO. What is the cause?

COURTIER (*he speaks in a shocked tone*): A disaster, Master Leonardo! The water pipes do not work! !
When her Excellence was pleased to take a bath this evening, the tap broke and the water would not flow! ! ! The Duchess is very wroth, and awaits your Worship's coming.

(*He steps aside, and bows*)

LEONARDO (*looking at his household, at the courtier, and at the open door*): Ah! The Duchess's bath!

(*He walks out past the bowing courtier*)

CURTAIN

CHRISTOPHER COLUMBUS

(age 12-13)

This play is simpler and more straightforward than the last, and concerns mainly the events on board the *Santa Maria* leading up to the first sighting of the Western World. The first scene is in the nature of a prologue. For the first time, however, we must have more elaborate scenery. The scene in the monastery can be performed in front of a traverse curtain which, when pulled aside, discloses the ship. This need only consist of the farther side of the ship's bulwark upon which the actors can lean and gaze seawards; the lower part of a mast, part of a sail and some rigging, in the centre, and on one side the poop with steering wheel. The backcloth can be blue, lit brightly for daylight and a deep blue for the night scene when a coloured lantern hung on the rigging makes an effective addition.

SCENE I

Guest Room of the Priory of La Rabida, near Palos, Spain. Table, Benches. Time: Autumn afternoon, 1484.
A loud knock is heard. It is repeated.
Enter lay-brother who crosses stage to answer the knock. Re-enter porter, followed by a tall man and a young boy. They are travellers and poorly clad.

TRAVELLER: We have left the highway to offer prayer at the shrine of Our Lady. Could you spare some milk and a loaf of bread for the boy?

PORTER *(smilingly nods assent. Exit)*

TRAVELLER: Sit, Diego.

(The traveller also sits and stares silently in front of him. Re-enter porter with bread and milk which he places beside the boy, who begins to eat hungrily)

PORTER: There is enough to spare for you, sir.

TRAVELLER: I thank you. *(He breaks off a piece of the loaf, but does not eat it, and resumes his seat)*

PORTER: You have travelled far?

TRAVELLER: From Lisbon.

PORTER: Lisbon! That is a great way. You are on foot?

TRAVELLER: Yes.

PORTER: You go much farther today?

TRAVELLER: To Palos—to the sea.

(Enter Father Alonzo)

ALONZO: Ah, we have guests! Whence come you sir? Are you a merchant?

TRAVELLER *(rising, still holding the uneaten bread in his hand and speaking in anger)*:
I am a mariner, born in Genoa, and because no-one will accept the kingdoms I offer, I have to beg my bread.

ALONZO *(laying his hand reassuringly on the other's shoulder and inviting him to sit down)*: You have a kingdom ... and yet ... so poor? Pray, tell me. ...

TRAVELLER: You would not understand. In all Portugal there was no one.

ALONZO: Nay, but perhaps ... a kingdom, you said? Far from here?

TRAVELLER: To the west—across the sea—where lie the rich lands of India and Cathay. To the *west*—do you understand? For I am one of those who hold that the world is round.

ALONZO *(nodding)*: I understand. I too am a geographer.

TRAVELLER *(turning to Alonzo for the first time)*: Till now, I have been mocked, scorned—and by those who know better—tricked. For fourteen years I have offered my plans to the Court at Lisbon—to Prince and King. But they spurned my offer and now I have left their country. I go to France.

ALONZO: Nay, but you must stay with us at least this night. The day is spent and you are surely weary. I would gladly hear more from you. ...

TRAVELLER (*rising*): You are kind. But we must press on. I seek a ship to take us both to France.

ALONZO: Why haste to France, since you are now in Spain? Our prior, Juan Perez, would gladly meet you. He is a man of learning and great understanding—and what is more, he knows the highest in the land. He was once the father-confessor to our Queen. He could give you letters. . . .

TRAVELLER: To Isabella and King Ferdinand?

ALONZO: Without a doubt. Come, let me show you our poor library. And I have maps. . . .

TRAVELLER (*as he follows Alonzo*): I had not thought of Spain!

CURTAIN (*leaving Diego, who has fallen asleep, his head on the table*)

SCENE II

At sea. October 1492. Early evening.
The stern poop is seen on the right. Sailors are seated about the deck. Two are gazing outward, leaning against the gunwale, with backs to audience. One of them speaks:

1ST SAILOR: Westward, ever westward! Does the wind blow *only* from the east?

2ND SAILOR: How then can we ever return? We shall be blown at length over the uttermost edge of the earth, into the abyss. So God will punish us.

3RD SAILOR: Aye, 'tis not right to venture thus into the unknown. We should be content to stay where God has placed us, within reach of our own shores.

4TH SAILOR: But the Admiral has told us that our earth is *round*.

5TH SAILOR (*jumping excitedly to his feet*): Aye—and are we not now sliding down the slope of it? How shall we ever climb up again—wind or no wind?

6TH SAILOR: That's what I say! And shall we not fall off? How can we hang upside down?

7TH SAILOR: What does the log say? How many leagues?

8TH SAILOR: Six hundred and fifty, by last night's reckoning.

7TH SAILOR: And so, a hundred still to go. Did not the Admiral swear he would not take us beyond seven hundred and fifty?

8TH SAILOR: That was his solemn promise. But 'tis my belief we have exceeded it—and still no sight of land!

9TH SAILOR: But we have seen birds. . . .

8TH SAILOR: Aye—but where are they now? 'Twas from some islands that they came, the Admiral said—islands no-one saw, but yet we passed them.

1ST SAILOR: Westward, ever westward. . . . And if the Admiral knew of these islands, why did he not put in at them? Answer me that!

3RD SAILOR: Let *him* answer it!

5TH SAILOR: We could still turn back.

2ND SAILOR: How could we—with this accursed wind out of the east?

6TH SAILOR: We could but try. . . . Better now than later, before we fall to perdition!

5TH SAILOR: Look, mates—let's be honest! Are we not all of one mind over this accursed voyage? Are we all to be driven into unknown horrors, to death and the devil?

CHORUS: Aye. We agree. Well spoken.

5TH SAILOR: Nay—but we refuse to die for the sake of this madman! Let's defy him! Turn the ship about, we say! Back to the islands! Seize the helm and 'bout ship!

CHORUS: Let's defy him! Turn the ship about. Back to the islands!

4TH SAILOR: Cowards! Would ye turn back now, having come thus far? Have ye no honour? No duty to the Queen?

6TH SAILOR: Honour's dead when oaths are broken! Did he not promise us land?

8TH SAILOR: Heed not the little sprat! Shall we be defied by a cabin boy?

7TH SAILOR: Throw him overboard!

4TH SAILOR: You don't dare!

6TH SAILOR: We'll dare more than that before we've done! Hold thy impudent tongue!

5TH SAILOR: What say you, comrades? Shall we summon the Admiral and tell him our demands?

6TH SAILOR: Nay—seize the helm and put him in chains!

CHORUS: Aye—to the devil with this madman. Put him in chains!

(*Enter Columbus on poop*)

COLUMBUS: What means this turmoil? Get ye to your beds. The day is done.

5TH SAILOR: You're no longer captain of this ship.

COLUMBUS: Is this mutiny? Know ye, that I am Admiral here by orders of their Majesties. Such words are treason!

CHORUS: Turn back the ship! We'll go no farther!

COLUMBUS: Who said that? All of you?

CHORUS: Aye—all of us!

COLUMBUS: If anyone thinks otherwise, let him show himself, and come up to me.

CHORUS: Nay—we are agreed, all of us!

4TH SAILOR: Not I, Sir! .... Let me go, I say! .... Not I, Sir, I am with you, Admiral!

(*He drags himself away from those who try to hold him, and leaps up on to the poop*)

COLUMBUS: Good, Fernando! Here then are two men against a score of curs!

5TH SAILOR: There's no use bluffing us, Admiral. We know what we want, and you are our prisoner.

COLUMBUS: And who then shall sail the ship home for you? And, if by some chance, ye find the coast of Spain, your welcome will be the gallows, for ye shall be strung up as traitors—every one of you—the moment ye set foot on shore. . . . Choose, then, 'twixt the gallows and my sword.

(*Drawing his sword*)

(*No one moves*)

COLUMBUS: I observe that ye all prefer the gallows. . . . But perchance ye may now be moved to reason. Have patience yet for three days—and if by then we find no land—ye may come to me again and speak of home. Do ye agree?

CHORUS: Three days?

COLUMBUS: I swear it. Get ye to bed.

8TH SAILOR: Nay, but we'll have no more of these promises! Shall we, men?

CHORUS: Nay, it's deeds we want, not promises. Turn the ship!

COLUMBUS: To turn the ship, ye must needs reach the wheel—and 'tis behind me. Which of you would wish to try?

(*The men try to push one another forward. The 5th sailor reaches the steps and draws a dagger*)

5TH SAILOR: Put up your sword, and surrender!

(*The steersman has left his wheel and creeps up behind Columbus, to seize him*)

FERNANDO: Admiral! The steersman! Behind you!

(*Columbus seizes the man by the arm, almost without looking round*)

COLUMBUS: Down, thou traitrous dog! (*He thrusts him down on to the deck below*)
Man the wheel, boy. The first to reach the poop is a dead man. . . . Likewise the second. . . . No one? Nevertheless, 'tis not my wish to make any man's wife a widow or his children fatherless, for have I not promised—as far as God will allow it—to bring you back safely to your homes? Grant me then this, that I need exert no violence on any of you . . . Get ye to bed.

(*The men slink off, one by one*)

Light the lantern, Fernando, and I shall take the wheel.

(*Fernando does so, as the curtain falls*)

CURTAIN

SCENE III

The same. The early morning of October 12th, 1492. Columbus is alone on deck, gazing seaward. He makes a sudden movement, as if he had seen something.

(*Enter Pedro Guttierez, a nobleman*)

COLUMBUS: (*without turning*): How are the crew, Pedro?

PEDRO: Quiet, but excited. They are all a-watch for land. They have seen today the branch of a tree floating by. They say tomorrow is the third day and you promised them land by the third day. . . .

COLUMBUS: I did . . . I pray God will be merciful . . . How calm the sea is! And the stars are veiled. Sometimes, on the edge of dawn, all nature holds her breath, and even time is poised and motionless . . . Look, Pedro—yonder. Dost thou see a light?

PEDRO: I do. It flickers red, then dies away. See, there it is again!

COLUMBUS: 'Tis like a torch, or fire. Surely there is land, if there is a light! Say naught—but bring Rodrigo . . . Surely there is land if there is light.

(*Pedro runs off and returns with Rodrigo Sanchez, the ship's treasurer*)

RODRIGO: A light? Where?

COLUMBUS: There!

RODRIGO: Nay, I see naught.

PEDRO: 'Tis gone . . . But we have seen it—red and flickering, like a fire . . . See, it comes again!

(*Voice off: A light, a light*)

COLUMBUS: The men have seen it!

(*Voices off: A light, a light! Enter number of crew, shouting excitedly*)

CREW: A light! Saw you the light, Sir? Can this be land?
A light! A light!

A boom of a gun: Shouts of, Land! Land ho! Land ho! as dawn breaks. The men cheer and shout wildly, rush to the rail and the poop. Then there is a hush, while one by one the men fall on their knees with Columbus, and chant

TE DEUM LAUDAMUS. . . .

CURTAIN

AFTER BATTLE

(age 13-14)

The next two plays are historical in the sense that they are based on real events which have taken place prior to the opening of the play. Thereafter the incidents, although purely imaginary, are typical of the kind of adventures which befell the two historical persons concerned, namely, King Charles II in the first play, and Prince Charles Edward (Bonny Prince Charlie) in the second, each during his escape to France after defeat in battle. In these two plays the attempt has been made to show the reactions of different people to the events of the time—in the first, the family split by opposing loyalties, and in the second, the loyalty and wit of highlanders in face of great danger.

CHARACTERS

MRS. PENDERLEIGH
OLIVER PENDERLEIGH, her son, a captain in Cromwell's army
RICHARD PENDERLEIGH, her younger son, an officer in the King's army
ANNE PENDERLEIGH, her daughter
A CAVALIER OFFICER
TOBIAS FARSIGHT, a puritan gentleman
KETURAH FARSIGHT, his wife
ABIGAIL FARSIGHT, his daughter
BETTY, maid to Mrs. Penderleigh
WILLIAM, a gardener, and soldier in the King's army
CORPORAL and TWO SOLDIERS of Cromwell's army

SCENE

A country house near Worcester, after the defeat of Charles II, September, 1651.

SCENE

The sitting-room of a country house of the seventeenth century. At the back is a recessed window, with a curtain to cover the recess. Through the window one sees the garden. *The room is simply but comfortably furnished, including a settle (left) and a table (right) on which are a flagon of wine, and glasses.*

It is late in a September afternoon. Betty the maid is busying herself about the room.

William rushes in, breathless and excited.

WILLIAM: Betty, Betty! The day is lost. Our cause is broken. . . . I come straight from the battle. . . . O, but you should have seen Master Richard . . . . how he led us—his horse prancing, his sword flashing, his helm glinting in the sun—and crying with a great voice: "Follow, men, follow, for God and King Charles!"

BETTY: And did you follow?

WILLIAM: Alas—I had no horse.

BETTY: Then—on foot?

WILLIAM: Aye—as best I could.

BETTY: And what had you for weapon, William? A pruning hook?

WILLIAM: Betty, 'tis no time for idle jesting. We must fly! I tell you, I saw it all.

BETTY: All?

WILLIAM: Aye—from a tree—'twas a mighty tall tree. . . . Nay 'tis no time for laughing. It was most perilous. Twice a musket-ball whistled in my ear. . . . All is lost Betty. The Scots are routed, the city has fallen, the King has fled.

BETTY: And what of Master Richard? Is he safe?

WILLIAM (*hurriedly*): I pray God so. . . . Now, let us away! The soldiery will be upon us.

BETTY: Fly? With you? And wherefore?

WILLIAM: This house is safe no longer for the likes of us. Betty, bethink you, it is a Royalist house!

BETTY: And what of that? You were a brave Cavalier this morning.

WILLIAM: Aye,—that was this morning,—but we must all be Roundheads now, or perish.

BETTY: Then fly if you will, you cowardly turn-coat! I will stay with my mistress.

WILLIAM: I'm not the only one in this house who has turned his coat. What of Master Oliver?

BETTY: Master Oliver is no longer a son of this house,—and that you know well. Be off with you!

Enter Mrs. Penderleigh. It is plain that she is agitated, but she is outwardly calm and dignified.

MRS. P.: There is news, Betty—bad news for us, I fear. There are many fugitives. Some may seek shelter in friendly houses. You understand? I rely upon the loyalty—and the discretion of my servants.

BETTY: Yes, Madam.

MRS. P.: And you, William, had best be busy about the garden.

(*William touches his forelock meekly, and goes out*)

Will you ask Mistress Anne to come to me here, Betty, and to fetch me my sewing?

(*Exit Betty. Mrs. Penderleigh looks out of the window*)

'Twere best to leave the curtains undrawn.

Enter Anne Penderleigh.

ANNE: Here is your sewing, Mother.

(*They both sit and begin to sew. They speak for the most part lightly, to hide the growing tension*)

MRS. P.: I have left the curtains undrawn, Anne, that our light may be a guide to friends, and that our foes may see we have nothing to hide.

ANNE: Betty is bringing the candles. . . . (*Betraying her anxiety*) I wish that we had news of Richard!

MRS. P.: The messenger said that he was alive and unhurt—before the last charge. We must wait—and hope. . . . (*Brightly*) They say His Majesty is safe. He left before the battle had ended. May God protect him!

ANNE: Whither will he go?

MRS. P.: To France, no doubt. Praise God, there are many loyal homes, both great and humble, where he will find food and shelter on his way.

ANNE (*rising and approaching window*): It grows dark. Richard is so long of coming.

MRS. P.: He will have much to do. We must be patient.

ANNE (*returning to her seat and resuming her calm*): How I wish that I had seen the King! They say he is both brave and charming—of a dark complexion.

MRS. P.: Your Father knew him as a lad—before that fated battle.... Your Father died for his father. Now it may be that.... Now Richard has fought for him ... But had I a dozen sons they should all have fought for him.

ANNE (*bending over her sewing*): One did not....

MRS. P.: (*bitterly*): Speak no more of him! He has forsaken our sacred cause and brought disgrace upon our family, upon the name of Penderleigh. He is no longer my son.

ANNE (*quietly*): I loved Oliver....

Enter Betty with candles which she places on the table.

MRS. P.: Leave the curtains undrawn, Betty. The day is not yet done.

BETTY: Peters has come from the town, Madam, where all is quiet, he says.

MRS. P.: Thank you Betty. That is all his news?

BETTY: Yes, Madam—except that there be many fleeing round the countryside and that Cromwell's men are seeking the King.

MRS. P.: (*laughing*); Then they waste their time, for he has been gone these three hours.... If any of the soldiery do come to the door, Betty, open to them courteously. We have naught to hide. I fear I have dropped my needle.

(*Betty stoops to look for needle. The window opens, and a Cavalier leaps in*)

CAVALIER: I ask your pardon, ladies. . . . I beg you, be not afraid. . . . I am a poor fugitive, as you see. . . . I had lost touch with my companions—we were being pursued—I saw the light in your window—

MRS. P.: I pray you, Sir, be seated. (*Seeing him glance at Betty*) Have no fear, Sir, my servants are all trustworthy.

CAVALIER: I thank you, Madam, but I shall not detain you. 'Tis but for a few minutes, until the rabble has passed.

ANNE: Nay, Sir, stay. 'Tis not safe for you to be abroad. We have just had word that they are scouring the countryside, seeking the King. The roads and fields are swarming with soldiery.

MRS. P.: Pray, rest awhile, Sir. We shall give you food—and a hiding place for the night.

(*Sound of loud knocking*)

BETTY: The soldiers, Madam! What shall we do?

MRS. P.: Here, Sir, in the window is your safest place, then, if need be you can escape by the way you came. (*He retires to window-recess*) Quickly—draw the curtains! (*Betty does so*) Now, Betty open the door!

Exit Betty. Mrs. Penderleigh and Anne resume their sewing.
Enter Oliver Penderleigh.

ANNE: Oliver!

MRS. P.: What brings you here, Sir?

OLIVER: To see my family.

MRS. P.: You do not reckon, Sir, that your family may not wish to see you.

ANNE (*protesting*): Mother!

MRS. P.: Do you come to insult us in this hour of your triumph?

OLIVER: I said that I come to see my family. Also, I deemed that I might be of some service to you.

MRS. P.: We have no wish to be served by a traitor!

OLIVER: Nevertheless, I deem it my duty to remain. I have orders to search this house. With your permission, my men will begin.

MRS. P.: (*with indignation and increasing emotion*): For whom do you search, Sir? Whom should you expect to find in this poor house—save perhaps your own brother, Richard, who—for aught we know—may lie dead upon the field at this very hour—slain by your rebels.

OLIVER: He has not yet returned?

MRS. P.: No, you have been disappointed of your prey.

OLIVER: I seek not for him—to do him harm—but for a dark-complexioned man called Charles Stuart.

MRS. P.: (*laughing*): Know you not he is gone these three hours and more?

OLIVER: For that cause we seek him. (*To soldiers off*) Begin the search, corporal. Question every servant.

MRS. P.: I can only add, Sir, that I consider this an outrage.

OLIVER (*with a stiff bow*): I regret it, Madam, as much as you do.

ANNE: (Moving between Oliver and the window) Must you search all the house, brother? you know well we could not harbour the King. Report has it that he left ere the battle was ended.

OLIVER: Every room and every corner, sister. I do not hearken to idle gossip.

ANNE: Then go with your men, I pray you, lest they do hurt to the servants, or violence to the house—

OLIVER: My men are orderly both in word and in deed. If you have naught to hide, you have naught to fear. Are you afraid of aught?

ANNE (*Hurriedly resuming her seat*): O, no, brother. . . .

(*Oliver moves towards window and is about to investigate when Betty enters. She grasps the situation at once and speaks in a loud voice to distract Oliver's attention*)

BETTY: Madam, here are a gentleman and his lady wishful to see you.

Enter Tobias Farsight, his wife, and young daughter. They are dressed in strict puritan fashion.

TOBIAS (*with great unction*): Peace be upon this house!

MRS. F. AND DAUGHTER (*meekly echoing in unison*): Peace be upon this house.

TOBIAS (*pompously and as if preaching a sermon*): You may wonder at our intrusion, Madam. We are wayfarers who have been overtaken by darkness. There are many bands of soldiery about, and I deemed it not safe for my wife and daughter. May we beg the shelter of your hospitable roof?

MRS. P.: This is not an inn, Sir, but these are troublous times, and all in distress are surely welcome.

TOBIAS: I thank you, Madam. My name is Tobias Farsight; this is my spouse, Keturah, and my daughter Abigail.

(*The wife and daughter curtsey*)

MRS. P.: I pray you be seated.

(*They all sit down stiffly and simultaneously upon the settle*)

You must be weary from your journey. . . . Some wine, Betty—and prepare supper. . . .

TOBIAS (*with protesting hands*): Nay, Madam, some water—and a little bread—will suffice.

MRS. F. AND ABIGAIL (*echoing*):—a little bread will suffice.

Exit Betty

MRS. P.: How came you by our house? For we are not on the highway.

TOBIAS: A soldier fellow joined us in the darkness and offered to be our guide—if we would but lend him a cloak and a hat. He told us that he knew of a hospitable house, and did lead us hither.

MRS. P.: Where is he now?

TOBIAS: In the courtyard, tending our horses.

(*Voices off: A spy, Captain, a spy!*)

Enter Corporal and two soldiers leading a man with a puritan hat and cloak.

CORPORAL: See, Sir,—whom we have found in the Courtyard, disguised as a gentleman's servant. . . . (*Pulls off hat and cloak*)—a Royalist officer!

MRS. P.: Richard!

TOBIAS: My guide, Madam! One of the sons of the Mammon of Unrighteousness! See how the just judgment of heaven is fallen upon the wicked!

OLIVER: I will deal with this prisoner, Corporal. You may go. (*Exeunt Corporal and soldiers.*) I must speak with this prisoner alone.

MRS. P. (*agitated, to Farsight*): You will find supper awaiting you in the adjoining room, good Sir, and beds are prepared for you. . . . I trust you will be comfortable.

TOBIAS (*rising simultaneously with his family*): We thank you, Madam. (*Turning to Richard with uplifted hand and in his most parsonic tone*) Young man, this day hath seen the vials of wrath poured upon the heads of the ungodly. Repent, my friend, repent!. . . . ere it be too late.

Exeunt Farsights in procession.

MRS. P.: Must we go also?

ANNE: Oliver—you will spare his life!

OLIVER: Richard's life is in his own and in God's hands,—not in mine. I would not willingly touch a hair of his head. . . . Retire now, and leave us.

MRS. P.: (*ignoring Oliver, crosses to Richard and grasps him by the hands*): Goodnight, Richard. God bless you! . . . Come, Anne.

Exeunt Mrs. P. and Anne.

RICHARD: Am I then a prisoner in my own house?

OLIVER: Better in your own house than elsewhere.

RICHARD: Bandy not words! You know I am no spy. I adopted this poor disguise only to escape to my own home. Is that a crime?

OLIVER: You are not accused of wearing a cloak and a hat, Richard, but of rebelling against the Commonwealth of England. In short, you are a traitor—and you know the punishment of traitors.

RICHARD: You lie! 'Tis you who are the traitor—to your King and your country! Quit my house this instant, you dog!

OLIVER: Not your house, I think, Richard—but mine: first, by reason of birth, I being the elder, and second by reason of your conduct, you being a rebel. The law would not support your claim, Richard.

RICHARD: Now I see the reason of your coming hither. You would use this day's victory to rob me of my patrimony! Our father struck your name from his will when you turned traitor to the King.

OLIVER: I hoped I should find you in a reasonable mind, Richard. . . . Every suspected house 'twixt here and Worcester is being searched for fugitives. I chose to search this one—so that those most near to me, my own flesh and blood—might be spared. As master of this house, I can take responsibility for those in it—if they be reasonable. But if you run your neck into a halter, Richard, I can do naught for you.

RICHARD: So, to save my neck I must foul my knees grovelling before you, Oliver, and kiss your puritanical feet! Not so long as I have breath in my body to cry: "God save his Majesty!" Come—you dog—we shall fight for this! (*Draws his sword*)

OLIVER (*drawing sword reluctantly*): Then your blood be upon your own head! But—ere we begin, Richard, remember—my death will only make certain your own. I should be right sorry for that.

RICHARD: Then at least we die together. . . . Come!

(*They fight. It is soon seen that Richard is the better swordsman, and he strikes Oliver's sword from his hand. He points to where the sword lies*)

Your sword brother.

OLIVER (*picking up his sword*): You play skilfully!

RICHARD: A Cavalier knows how to handle his sword.

(*The fight is resumed. Oliver is hard pressed. Richard fights fanatically, and it is plain that he is winning. Suddenly the window curtain opens and the Cavalier steps out. He seizes Richard's arm)*

CAVALIER: Stay! This day hath seen bloodshed enough. Put up your swords, gentlemen. I would gladly help settle your quarrel in a more peaceful manner, and for this you may count me at your service. (*He speaks as one accustomed to be obeyed, but with an easy debonair manner)*

OLIVER: Who are you, Sir, and whence came you?

CAVALIER: Egad! from behind this curtain. I have been prisoned there this half an hour, for neither could I come in because of you nor go out because of your men. So I have been an unwilling auditor of your little family dispute.

OLIVER: Fool that I was, not to search that corner!

CAVALIER: 'Twas good you did not, Sir, for then I should not have been there to save your life.... But let us be brief, for my time is short.... Master Richard, you indeed owe your life to your brother, for without him you would be hanged. You, Master Oliver, owe your life to me, I think. Repay me by granting one small request and I shall make all right for you 'twixt you and your brother.

OLIVER: What is your request?

CAVALIER: Only that you call off your men in the garden, there, until such time as you no longer hear the sound of my horse's hooves upon the highway.

OLIVER: (*reluctantly*): Since I owe my life to you, I must grant your request.

CAVALIER: Go then. I shall await your return.

Exit Oliver

RICHARD: Your Majesty! (*throwing himself on his knees and kissing the Cavalier's hand*) Let me go with you, Sire! Let me follow you for ever!

CAVALIER (*with great kindness*): No, my young friend. I go but from danger to danger. I have snatched you from one death. Run not

AFTER BATTLE

so soon into another. Stay here, be reconciled with your brother—for, in truth he loves you—and one day—God willing—I shall return to my kingdom. In that day, I shall need my friends. Till then, be at peace.

RICHARD: God bless and protect Your Majesty!

CAVALIER (*Hearing Oliver returning*): Hush!

(*Richard rises quickly*)

Enter Oliver

OLIVER: My men are withdrawn.

CAVALIER: I thank you. Your brother has promised me to be at peace with you and to place himself in your care—(*looking meaningfully at Richard*)—until such time as I shall release him from his promise. Does that suffice? (*Oliver nods assent*) Then, ere I go do you clasp each other by the hand. (*They do so, and for a moment the Cavalier lays his hand warmly on theirs*)
Goodbye—and good fortune attend you both! (*He goes through the window.*)

RICHARD: Good luck to you, Sir!

(*Richard walks quietly to the table and pours out two glasses of wine*)

Listen!

(*The sound of hooves is heard, growing fainter, till it dies away*)

He is gone. . . . Now, Oliver, will you drink a toast with me?

OLIVER: Right gladly, Richard. What is your toast?

RICHARD (*raising his glass*): To the good fortune of this house and to the health and long life of our friend the Cavalier!

OLIVER: With all my heart! (*They drink*)

RICHARD (*Laughing*): Now, Oliver, I have you in my power!

OLIVER: How so?

RICHARD: You have drunk the health of His Majesty the King!

OLIVER: The King!!

CURTAIN

BONNY JUSTICE

(age 13-14)

In this play it should be noted that three different accents are used—that of the Highland folk who speak English but with a Highland accent, that of the English officer and his men, and that of one character who speaks broad Lowland Scots. Whoever produces the play should therefore be acquainted with both the Highland and Lowland accents. (See also notes on the play under "After Battle".) All the Highlanders wear the kilt, and the Lowlander the ordinary clothes of an eighteenth century serving man.

Scene: Inn in a small Highland village
Time: Summer of 1746, after the battle of Culloden.

(*Two men drinking at table; Catriona, and Morag Macdonald*)

1ST VILLAGER: And where would you be going, Morag, last Saturday evening?

MORAG: Och, I was taking a walk.

1ST VILLAGER: But was it not with Shamus McDougall that I saw you, down by the bridge?

MORAG: Maybe you did.

2ND VILLAGER: Did I not hear there was a croft to be let, Donal', somewhere up the glen?

1ST VILLAGER: Och well now, and is that not a good thing for you, Morag,—but I would be sorry for you to be leaving the old inn.

MORAG: You need not be worrying, Donal'. I will not be leaving the old inn. Your head is just full of your marriages,—and you an old man. And it is always other people's weddings you are planning. It is a pity you did not show a good example to the clachan and take a wife for yourself.

2ND VILLAGER: Did you ever hear of a doctor who would be taking his own physic, Morag?

CATRIONA: Morag does not need to be going up the glen for her "physic". There are folk nearer at hand . . .

(*Enter Rabbie Ramsay*)

MORAG: Surely you do not need to be putting in your tongue along with the men, Catriona. They are quite foolish enough.

1ST VILLAGER: Well, I will be going, Morag, since you have not the appreciation for my talk.

2ND VILLAGER: Will you tell your mother that I will be bringing down the calf on Friday, Morag.

MORAG: I will.

(*Exeunt villagers*) Here are your eggs, Catriona.

(*Exit Catriona*)

Will you bring in the peats, Rabbie?

RABBIE: Afore I bring in the peats—wull ye mairry me, Morag?

MORAG: No, not before you bring in the peats.

RABBIE: Then,—efter—wull ye listen tae me?

MORAG: Is this a time to be listening to such talk—with "himself" hunted like a thief from clachan to clachan, and from glen to glen?

RABBIE: Morag, Morag,—wull ye no be din thinking aboot Cherlie, and gie a bit thocht tae me? Forby,—hae I no' speired ye mony a time thae twal' month syne?

MORAG: It is these twelve months that I am thinking of other things. . . .

RABBIE: Hae a' ye weemen gan' gyte? Maun the hale warld stap gaen' roon'—maun a' thing cam' tae an end—maun there be nae mair mairryin' an' gien in mairriage—syne the year seventeen hunner and fowerty-five?

MORAG: You are a stranger here, Rabbie, and a Lowlander, and you do not understand.

RABBIE: Aye,—I'm a Lowlander—an' no' sic a stranger either,—but I'm thinkin' that I unnerstaund gey weel. . . . Morag,—dae ye lo'e me?

MORAG: Rabbie, I think I do . . . Next to himself . . . yes, I think I do, Rabbie.

RABBIE: Next tae himsel'! Next tae himsel'! The bonny pouthered Frenchy! . . . But whit guid is he tae ye noo?—a rinawa', an ootlaw,—a puir landless, penniless, feckless loon! Forby—ye canna *a'* mairry him!

MORAG: And what are *you* at all but a poor, landless, penniless, feckless loon? And how do I know that you are not a runaway and an outlaw yourself? What are you doing here in the highlands, I ask you? . . . Have you a house or land to offer me, or silver in your stocking? Or is it the inn you are thinking to be marrying as well as myself?

RABBIE: Gin I had ma richts, it's baith land and a hoose I'd hae,—for I'm a laird's son, Morag,—but they hae ta'en ma faither's land. He was oot in the "15" wi' Jamie—bad cess tae the hale clamjamfray o' Stuarts,—an' I was born a puir man's son,—aye, and an ootlaw, gin ye wull. But it's no' innkeeping I'd be daen, Morag,—an' I wudna tak' yer auld rubble o' a hoose in a gift!

(*Exit to kitchen*)

(*Enter Shamus McDougall*)

(*Takes a seat at table while Morag brings him drink*)

MORAG: Have you any news, Shamus?

SHAMUS: He is being passed westward from one glen to the next always with a guide who knows his own country,—and so to the water, and a boat.

MORAG: He will be going back to France? There is no more hope?

SHAMUS (*shakes his head sadly*): They are lying at Culloden in their thousands,—and the rest are scattered like stirks on a mountain-side.

MORAG: But surely he will come again . . . About where will he be now?

SHAMUS: Even if I was to be knowing where he will be now, the word must not be spoken.

(*Enter Dougal Cameron. He remains standing with his back to the door*)

DOUGAL: Is your mother in the house, Morag? I would be speaking with her.

MORAG (*towards right*): Mother,—Mother! Here is Dougal Cameron—to speak with you. . . . Do you sit down, Dougal.

(*Enter Mrs. Macdonald*)

DOUGAL: Mrs. Macdonald (*glancing at Shamus, who has risen*) I have to bring the word to you . . . Himself will be here tonight . . . You will have a hiding-place? He will leave before the dawn. It is myself will be taking him on the next step.

MORAG: Tonight? O, Mother! But can we not give him a bed? He will be weary . . .

MRS. MACDONALD: A bed—but in the straw, Morag,—in the loft above the stable,—for there are eyes everywhere—and ears as well—and this is an inn . . . Tell Rabbie to spread fresh straw, and do you put the pot on the fire,—quickly! (*Exit Morag*) Is he being followed close?

DOUGAL: There were red-coats in Glen Sherrach, but he slipped through them in the dark. That is all I know.

MRS. MACDONALD: And his friends—where are they? He is not alone?

DOUGAL: They had to separate in the dark to avoid the red-coats, but his guide, Mackinnon, is with him, and they have been hiding all this day in a wood. Mackinnon crept up to the clachan at dusk to look for a man who would know the country and who could be taking him farther tomorrow.

MRS. MACDONALD (*beginning to prepare the table for supper*): And you will be coming, when?

DOUGAL: An hour before dawn.

MRS. MACDONALD: You will wait at the stable. Rabbie will waken him, with food for the day. (*Going to kitchen door*) Morag—will you lay the table now? Rabbie,—peats for the fire! Shamus—you will speak no word in the clachan.

SHAMUS: I am watchful over my tongue, Mrs. Macdonald.

(*Enter Morag with dishes and Rabbie with peat*)

MRS. MACDONALD: Then I will bid you both good-night.

(*A knock at the door, which Dougal opens*)

(*In the doorway appears Prince Charles, and behind him Roderick Mackinnon. They step in*)

MACKINNON: This is Mrs. Macdonald, Your Highness . . .

CHARLES (*extending a gracious hand*): Ah, Mrs. Macdonald . . .

(*Mrs. Macdonald and Morag curtsey, Shamus and Dougal kneel, while Rabbie stands staring*)

(DIM OUT)

(*When lights go up, Charles is at the table having just finished supper. Only Mrs. Macdonald and Morag are with him*)

MORAG: Would Your Highness wish for some more?

CHARLES: No more, I thank you. An excellent supper, I do assure you, Miss Morag. I thank you on behalf of both of us. Mackinnon has not yet returned from his stroll, but I am weary and would gladly sleep. So now, where shall we bestow ourselves?

MRS. MACDONALD: In the loft above the stable, if it please Your Highness. We have better beds, but none safer. I hope Your Highness will find it comfortable. I will call Rabbie to take you there. He is a faithful servant, and he will waken Your Highness in the morning.

CHARLES: I do thank you, Mrs. Macdonald. I have slept in *many* a worse place these many days past. And now (*taking her by the hand*) my thanks to you, my dear and noble lady, for your great kindness, and for the risk you have run for my sake . . . and to you, Miss Morag . . .

(*Enter Mackinnon*)

MACKINNON: Your Highness, there is a party of redcoats coming up the glen!

CHARLES: How far away?

MACKINNON: Not above half a mile.

CHARLES: It seems, Mrs. Macdonald, I shall not be able to accept of your kind hospitality after all. I must take to the hills again, Mackinnon,—and at all speed.

MACKINNON: I shall attend Your Highness.

MRS. MACDONALD: Sir, the night is dark. There is no moon.

CHARLES: The better for me, dear lady!

MRS. MACDONALD: Your Highness cannot do it. You do not know the country, Mackinnon. There is dangerous bog,—and there is no time. You will fall into their very arms, if you do not drown in the bog.

CHARLES: But I have no other course, Mrs. Macdonald. If I am taken, I am taken; but for your sake, good lady, I would not wish it to be in your house.

MRS. MACDONALD: Will you be listening to me, all of you! This is the last house in the clachan. If they pass this door, then all is well. But if they turn in here, they will be looking in every corner, and there will be only one place where Your Highness will be hiding.

CHARLES: And where should that be?

MRS. MACDONALD: In this very room, and under their very noses. Morag—tell Rabbie to take His Highness to the loft and then let Rabbie return to the kitchen. If the soldiers stop here, he must take the word at once to His Highness, and then they must *exchange clothes*. Rabbie will then run over the hill to McEachan's farm, till morning, and His Highness will be serving here in his place. Your name will be—Donald—Donald McLeod—from Barra, if it please Your Highness.

CHARLES: I place myself entirely in your hands, good lady.

MORAG: This way, Sir.

(Exit Charles and Morag to kitchen)

MRS. MACDONALD: Mackinnon, you will go to the house of Dougal Cameron, by the bridge, and give him the word. And it would be better for you to remain there for the night, letting this place be empty.

MACKINNON: I will. *(Exit)*

(Mrs. Macdonald draws up chairs to table and arranges room. Enter Morag)

MORAG: I have told Rabbie. They have gone to the stable. What must I be doing now?

MRS. MACDONALD: You will be waiting here, Morag, and see that Rabbie does not leave the kitchen. He must not be seen by the redcoats. When they come, you will call for me and then you will go at once to the kitchen and tell Rabbie. I will keep them in talk while Rabbie goes to the stable,—and for the changing of the clothes. Then himself must come in by the back door and be ready to come when I will be calling him.

MORAG: O mother—but I am—I am—afraid for him.

MRS. MACDONALD: This is not a time to be talking about such a thing.

(Exit)

(Enter Rabbie)

MORAG: Rabbie! You must not come here. You must not be seen. Go back at once!

RABBIE: I ha'e ta'en him tae his stable, and there he maun bide! As for bein' seen, certes I'll be seen, and tae some purpose. There's a price o' thirty thoosand pund upon his heid, and afore this nicht's ower, that pickle siller sall be *mine*. Through Jamie, ma faither lost his land. Through Charlie, I'll buy it back again. Is that no' bonny justice?

MORAG: Rabbie! You don't mean ... Rabbie!

RABBIE: Certes, I mean it! And dae ye think I'd be hiding yonder in Cherlie's kilts, and get masel' hangit for helping him tae escape? ... I may be a Lowlander, but I'm no' *that* gleckit!

MORAG: Rabbie,—you have asked me to marry you.

RABBIE: Aye,—but ye said ye lo'ed me *efter* himsel'. When Cherlie's awa' maybe I'll be *first* on yer list.

MORAG: Do you think I could be marrying a traitor?

RABBIE: When I hae that siller in ma pooch, Morag, it's near ony lady in the land I can be mairrying, and maybe ye'll no' be askit.

MORAG: The soldiers may be here at any moment. Rabbie—this young life—how could you let it be taken? Would you be a murderer? It is not *his* blame that your father lost his land!

RABBIE: Is it no' written in the scriptures that the sins o' the faithers sall be veesited on the bairns unto the third and fourth generation?

MORAG: I will ask you only one thing, for I see that your mind is made up. Will you do at least what my mother has asked,—lend him your clothes and send him here? ... I want no bloodshed ... You are forgetting that at the moment he is armed. He will certainly defend himself, and the first ball from his pistols might be for his betrayer ... That would be a pity, now. But in your clothes—and unarmed—he would be more easily taken, would he not? It is you who would be having the pistols.

RABBIE: What ye say is true. There can be nae hairm in that. Indeed, it would be better that way.

MORAG: Then it is agreed. What *you* will do, will lie upon your own head.

(*Loud knock at door. Exit Rabbie. Morag opens door*)
(*Enter Captain Joyce and Soldiers*)

JOYCE: Can I have entertainment here for myself and my men?

MORAG: Certainly, sir.

JOYCE: Then bring us supper and ale. (*They sit at table*)

MORAG: Mother, here are six gentlemen for supper.

(*Enter Mrs. Macdonald*)

MRS. MACDONALD: Good evening, gentlemen. Pray make yourselves at home. (*To Morag*) Tell Donald to draw fresh ale (*Exit Morag*) You have travelled far today?

JOYCE: Some twenty miles.

MRS. MACDONALD: That is far enough in these parts, where the roads are so wild.

JOYCE: Do you have many strangers passing this way?

MRS. MACDONALD: O Sir, very few. So we are glad to welcome them when they come and to hear news of the country beyond the glen.

JOYCE: I was hoping to hear some news from *you*, Ma'am. An inn-keeper usually hears all the gossip of the countryside.

MRS. MACDONALD: O yes, Sir,—gossip indeed,—but not such as would be interesting to you, Sir . . . Hector's cow is sick,—or Allistair's sheep are in a snowdrift—and now and again a marriage, or maybe there is a quarrel to be hearing about . . .

JOYCE: You have heard, I suppose, of the battle at Culloden?

MRS. MACDONALD: We did, indeed, Sir.

JOYCE: How long did that news take to reach you?

MRS. MACDONALD: It would be perhaps a fortnight, for news travels quickly at such a time. The men will be running with the word from one glen to the next.

JOYCE: And perhaps some returning from the battle?

MRS. MACDONALD: That could be.

JOYCE: You will have heard, no doubt, that Prince Charles Edward escaped after the battle?

MRS. MACDONALD: That I can well believe, Sir.

JOYCE: And we have now some reason to believe that he is somewhere in hiding in this glen.

MRS. MACDONALD: In this glen, Sir! Now, that *would* be news indeed!

(*Enter Charles with the ale*)

JOYCE: We intend to search this village thoroughly, so you will not mind if we examine this house? We have a warrant to do this, in the king's name.

MRS. MACDONALD: O, not at all, Sir. It is not a large house, but you can look at every corner of it.

JOYCE: The remainder of my men are searching the other houses now, and they have orders to bring here every man and woman whom they find, so that I may question them. You will not mind that I abuse your hospitality in this way?

MRS. MACDONALD: O no, Sir.

JOYCE: You will then also bring your own household into this room, while some of my men search this house.

MRS. MACDONALD: As you please, Sir. I have only Morag, my daughter, and my servingman, Donald.

(*The door is thrown open and villagers enter, followed by soldiers*)

JOYCE: Ah, here they come,—You two—search this house.

(*Exeunt two soldiers*)

MRS. MACDONALD: Donald, will you fetch Morag from the kitchen.

(*Exit Charles, returning at once with Morag*)

JOYCE: Anything to report, sergeant?

SERGEANT: Nothing, Sir. We think he must have passed on. But I have left men on guard.

JOYCE: Good. We must search the hills at daybreak. Now, I wish for you all to stand round the room so that I may see you;—and answer my questions, in the King's name ... You, fellow (pointing to Charles) What is your name?

CHARLES (*in highland accent*): Donald McLeod, Sir.

JOYCE: Do you belong to this village?

CHARLES: I come from Barra.

JOYCE: Hm. Where's that? Never heard of it.

CHARLES: It is an island, Sir.

JOYCE: You are a servant in this inn. Have you ever seen anyone known to you to be, or who might possibly be, Charles Edward Stuart, pass through this village?

CHARLES: No, Sir. I have seen no one of that description *pass through* this village.

JOYCE: You swear to this?

CHARLES: I swear it, Sir.

JOYCE: Now,—you! (*pointing to an old man*). Your name?

OLD MAN (*very deaf*): What does he say?

JOYCE: *Your name!*

VILLAGERS: He is asking your *name!*

OLD MAN: I am Allistair McAllistair.

JOYCE: What is your occupation?

OLD MAN: Eh?

JOYCE: *What is your occupation?* (*Old Man shakes his head*) (*to villagers*) What does he *do?*

OLD MAN: Och, she is not doing well at all, she is dead.

JOYCE: *Who* is dead?

CATRIONA: It is his cow.

JOYCE: It is his *what*?

(*A musket shot is heard outside*)

(*Door bursts open and two soldiers rush in*)

1ST SOLDIER: We have him, Sir!

JOYCE: Who?

2ND SOLDIER: Charles Edward! Shot dead, Sir!

(Joyce rushes out. A soldier is holding a lantern over the body of Rabbie Ramsay. Joyce stoops down and searches the dead man's pockets. He returns to the room, holding a letter)

JOYCE: 'Tis he indeed. This letter from his pocket proves it, Sergeant. His face, I fear, is too much injured . . . Who fired the shot?

1ST SOLDIER: I did, Sir. He was about to enter. He had pistols in his hands, and I feared for your safety.

JOYCE: He was a bold man to face such odds. You may go, good people.

(Villagers file out and soldiers carry away body)

We shall return anon for supper.

(Exit Joyce)

(Mrs. Macdonald, Morag and Charles stand staring at one another)

MORAG: It was Rabbie. He was going to betray Your Highness—for the sake of the money . . . I knew he would come . . . so I slipped out and told a soldier to be watching at our door . . . It was the only way . . . Your Highness will have plenty of time to escape . . . before they discover . . . their mistake.

(Morag collapses)

CURTAIN

THREE FRENCH SKETCHES

LE PETIT PARESSEUX

This is in rhyme and is suitable for younger children, age about 9. It tells of a little boy who would not get up in the morning and of his parents' ruse to get him out of bed. In the centre of the stage is the little boy in bed, and in one corner a breakfast table at which father and mother are seated. Alternately they walk across to speak to the boy, and then return to the table as if it were in another room.

MAMAN: Lève-toi, lève-toi, Pierre!
  Voilà le soleil qui brille.
  Lève-toi, lève-toi, Pierre,
  Il est sept heures et demie.

PIERRE: Je n'ai pas bien dormi,
  Et Maman, j'ai sommeil.
  Je n'ai ancune envie
  De regarder le soleil.

MAMAN: Si tu ne feras pas
  Tout ce que je te dis,
  Je t'enverrai Papa,
  Et tu seras puni.

PIERRE: Je n'ai pas peur de Papa,
  Car sous mon édredon
  Personne ne pourra
  Me donner du bâton.

PAPA: Que fait ce garçon-là
  Qui dort toujours si bien?

PIERRE: En verité, Papa,
  Je ne fais rien.

PAPA: Tu seras fouetté
  Si tu restes au lit.

PIERRE (*se cachant sous les draps*): Papa, en verité,
　Je ne suis pas ici.

PAPA (*à Maman*): J'ai cherché le garçon.
　Hélas, personne n'y est.
　Il faut que nous mangeons
　Son petit déjeuner.

PIERRE: Papa, Maman chérie,
　Ne vous dérangez plus.
　J'ai bien changé d'avis.
　Me voici revenu!

AU CAFÉ

This second sketch, suitable for age 12 or 13, is a scene in a café with father, mother, a very spoilt little boy and a very self-righteous little girl.

MAMAN: Pas de place, mon ami, pas de place!

PAPA: Mais oui, ma chérie . . . Voilà une table libre là-bas.

PIERRE (à *haute voix*): Puis-je avoir une glace, Papa?

MAMAN: Chut! pas maintenant. Tais-toi!

PIERRE: Tu m'as promis une glace, Maman!

MARIE: Tais-toi! Tu n'es pas poli.

(*Ils s'asseyent*)

PAPA: Qu'est-ce que tu veux, ma chérie?

PIERRE: Je veux une glace, du chocolat, de la limonade, des gâteaux, des bonbons.

PAPA: Tais-toi! Je parle à ta mère.

MARIE: Tais-toi! Tu n'es pas poli.

MAMAN: J'aimerais du café, , , , Qu'est-ce que tu veux, Marie?

MARIE: Je veux de la limonade, Maman, s'il te plaît.

GARÇON: Bonjour Madame, bonjour Monsieur. Qu'est-ce que vous désirez?

PAPA: Deux cafés et deux limonades, s'il vous plaît.

PIERRE (à *haute voix*): Et pour moi une glace, du chocolat, de la limonade, des gâteaux, des bonbons . . .

PAPA: Non, non, Pierre. C'est trop. Nous allons déjeuner tout à l'heure.

MARIE: Oui, c'est trop. Tu n'es pas poli. Moi, je suis polie, n'est-ce pas, Maman?

MAMAN: Oui, Marie, tu es toujours polie.

PIERRE: Mais tu m'as promis une glace, Papa!

PAPA: Pas maintenant, Pierre.

PIERRE (*en pleurant*): Mais tu m'as promis une glace, tu m'as promis une glace, tu m'as *promis* une glace . . .

   (*Le garçon arrive avec le café et la limonade sur un plateau*) Voilà! (*Pierre frappe le plateau. Les verres et les tasses tombent et se cassent. Le café et la limonade sont renversés sur la robe d'une dame*)

MAMAN: Je vous demande pardon, Madame. C'était un accident.

DAME (*furieuse*): Un accident, Madame! Votre fils a frappé le plateau. Je l'ai vu! C'est un méchant garçon, un enfant terrible! un enfant tout à fait gâté!

MAMAN: Pardon, Madame, c'est un enfant sage, et très bien élevé.

DAME: Bien élevé! Je l'ai vu! Il a frappé le plateau!

MAMAN: Je vous dis, Madame, c'était un accident!

GARÇON: Monsieur, voulez-vous payer les tasses et les verres? Ils sont cassés.

PAPA: Non, non, C'était un accident. Je ne paiérai rien,—ni le café ni la limonade non plus!

GARÇON: Pardon, Monsieur, mais il faut payer . . .

DAME: Ma belle robe est abimée, Madame. Vous devez me payer quelque chose . . .

MAMAN: Je ne vous paiérai rien, Madame. . . . Allons, mon ami . . . Il est presque midi . . . Il faut déjeuner . . .

   (*La famille sort*)

MARIE (*en sortant*): Et moi, je suis toujours polie, n'est-ce pas, Maman?

   (*La dame, le garçon et les autres clients les regardent*)

LA TANTE HÉLÈNE

This is also suitable for age 12 to 13 and deals with a mother, her five children, and the visit of an impossible aunt.

All three sketches should be played with verve, and can be tremendous fun.

MAMAN: Alors, mes enfants, écoutez bien. C'est aujourd'hui que vient votre tante Hélène. Elle arrive tout à l'heure. Nous ne l'avons pas vue depuis quinze ans. C'est la soeur de Papa,—une dame très aimable et tout à fait charmante. Il faut que vous soyez toujours polis—vous comprenez?—très, très polis. Vous vous êtes lavé les mains?

ENFANTS: Oui, Maman.

MAMAN: Et Pierre—les oreilles! Laisse-moi regarder. Bien! Et qu'est-ce que vous dites quand la tante Hélène vous parle?

ENFANTS: "Oui, ma tante," "Non, ma tante", "s'il te plaît, ma tante".

MAMAN: Très bien. Et si la tante vous apporte des cadeaux?

ENFANTS: "Oh, merci bien, ma tante! Tu es bien aimable!"

(*On sonne*)

MAMAN: Marie! On sonne! Vite—la porte!

(*La tante Hélène entre avec sa femme de chambre qui est si chargée de valises et de cartons à chapeau, qu'on ne peut pas voir son visage*)

TANTE: Ah, ma chère Amélie, quel voyage! Je suis tout à fait épuisée.

MAMAN: Assieds-toi, ma chère Hélène. Veux-tu du café?

TANTE: Oh, oui. J'en voudrais bien. Et du gâteau. J'ai une faim de loup.

MAMAN: Marie—du café et du gâteau, s'il vous plaît . . . Mais—cette dame-ci?

TANTE: Oh, ça—c'est ma femme de chambre. Je ne peux pas voyager sans ma femme de chambre. Dis à ta bonne de lui montrer ma chambre et une chambre pour elle.

MAMAN: Mais—je n'ai qu'une chambre libre, ma chère Hélène... il y a les enfants...

TANTES: Les enfants? Combien d'enfants as-tu?

MAMAN: Les voilà... J'en ai cinq.

TANTE: Cinq enfants! Ce sont *tous* tes enfants! Je croyais que c'étaient des visiteurs! Cinq enfants! C'est trop, c'est impossible! Que fait-on avec cinq enfants?

MAMAN: Ça fait beaucoup de travail, certainement, et il faut aussi beaucoup de chambres.

TANTE: Oh, ces petites affaires s'arrangeront. Deux ou trois enfants peuvent se coucher au salon, n'est-ce pas?... Louise, allez à la cuisine et dites à la bonne que nous avons besoin de deux chambres. Et vous—les enfants—vous voudriez bien dormir au salon ou dans la salle à manger, n'est-ce pas?

ENFANTS: Oh, oui, ma tante.

MAMAN: Mais je ne sais que faire! Nous n'avons pas assez de lits!

TANTE: Oh, des lits! N'importe! Les enfants n'ont pas besoin de lit! On se couche par terre, par exemple,—ou sur le canapé... Ah, voici mon café, et le gâteau! (*Marie entre avec le café*)

ENFANTS: Maman, puis-je dormir au salon? Moi... moi... moi— s'il te *plaît*, Maman!

MAMAN: Chut! Soyez polis, mes enfants. Ne faites pas tant de bruit!

TANTE: Oh quel bruit! J'aurai mal à la tête avec tout ce fracas!

PIERRE: Ma tante,—qu'y a-t-il dans toutes ces boîtes-là? Est-ce que ce sont des cadeaux pour nous?

TANTE: Des cadeaux?

ENFANTS: Oh merci bien, ma tante. Tu es bien aimable!

TANTE: Je ne suis pas aimable. Toutes ces boîtes sont pour moi. Je n'ai pas de cadeaux, et je n'aime pas les enfants. Allez-vous-en, et jouez quelque part—mais pas ici. Allez jouer dans la chambre d'enfants. Tes enfants, Amélie, ne savent-ils pas jouer comme tous les autres enfants? Sont-ils *toujours* au salon?

MAMAN: Mais non, Hélène,—mais notre chambre d'enfants—c'est maintenant *ta* chambre. Nous n'en avons plus.

TANTE: *Ma* chambre—une chambre pour jouer, pour tout un *village* d'enfants!

FEMME: (Laissant tomber toutes les boîtes par terre) Madame, je ne peux pas me tenir ici plus longtemps. Il n'y a pas de place ici pour moi. Je vais chez ma soeur. Elle habite cette ville. Ce n'est pas ainsi qu'on agit avec une femme de chambre. Au revoir Madame!

TANTE: Voilà ce que tu as fait, Amélie! Tu as chassé ma femme de chambre!

MAMAN: Moi? Je n'ai rien fait, Hélène. Je n'ai rien dit!

TANTE: Rien? Et tu lui as refusé une chambre—un lit même!

MAMAN: Mais—je ne peux pas donner ce que je ne possède pas! C'est impossible!

TANTE: Mais si! C'est tout à fait possible. J'ai dit que les enfants peuvent se coucher au salon, n'est-ce pas? Et maintenant tout est ruiné. J'ai perdu ma femme de chambre. Je suis désolée, au désespoir!

PIERRE: Peut-être on peut te trouver un bon hôtel, ma tante!

TANTE: Un hôtel! Mais comment porter à un hôtel tous ces bagages-là?

ENFANTS: Nous les transporterons, ma tante! Ce n'est rien!

(*Ils ramassent tous les bagages et sortent*)

MAMAN: Maintenant tu vois, ma chère Hélène, ce qu'on peut faire avec cinq enfants!

CURTAIN